RELIGION AND REVELATION

RELIGION
AND REVELATION

*A Study of Some Moments
in the effort of Christian Theology to define
their Relations*

Being the Paddock Lectures for 1931

BY

A. L. LILLEY

*Canon Residentiary,
Chancellor and Praelector of Hereford*

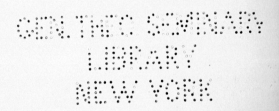

LONDON
SOCIETY FOR PROMOTING CHRISTIAN KNOWLEDGE
NORTHUMBERLAND AVENUE, W.C.2
NEW YORK: THE MACMILLAN COMPANY

First published 1932

Printed in Great Britain

TO THE HONOURED MEMORY OF

TWO GREAT MASTERS

IN THEOLOGY

GEORGE SALMON   JOHN GWYNN

CONTENTS

PREFACE

THIS little book contains the six lectures which I delivered in the month of December 1931, on the Lecture Foundation established in the General Theological Seminary of New York in memory of Bishop Paddock. To them I have prefixed an introductory summary suggesting a somewhat wider scope inherent in the subject I had chosen for treatment, and added a chapter more fully explanatory of my own position.

The lectures were the occasion of my second visit to America after an interval of more than a quarter of a century. Whatever changes I may have found in the outward appearance of things in that land of vigorous youth, with its impressive achievement and unbounded possibilities, the frankness and charm of its hospitality were unchanged, as indeed they seem unchangeable. It is quite impossible for me to acknowledge as I should like the innumerable kindnesses which made every day of my stay at the Seminary an experience to which I shall always look back with pleasure and gratitude. I hope my friends there will believe that I am thinking of them all when I recall with peculiar esteem and affection their Dean, Hughell Fosbroke, who has done and is doing so much to make the General Seminary a centre of the highest type of theological learning.

It was also a great privilege to meet in conference during a memorable week a group of the younger clergy from all parts of the States at the College of Preachers at Washington. To Bishop Rhinelander, whose largeness of vision created an institution in many ways unique and under whose wise guidance it is so successfully realising a fine idea, I most heartily offer my thanks for giving me this privilege.

Finally, I would thank the Provost of Trinity College, Toronto, my fellow-countryman and member of my own University, the Rev. F. H. Cosgrave, for his invitation to lecture at Trinity College during my stay on the other side of the Atlantic. It gave me my first opportunity of visiting a Dominion to the upbuilding of which so many of my fellow-Ulstermen have contributed. Naturally I felt at home there. It was as if I had just crossed to Belfast.

A. L. LILLEY.

August 2, 1932.

INTRODUCTORY

THE chief difficulties about religion which are felt with a peculiar acuteness in our day, whether by the learned or among the multitude, would seem to centre upon two points : (1) the fact and nature of Revelation, and (2) the apparent opposition or at least serious conflict between certain attributes which for philosophy are implied in the very idea of a Divine Being and certain others which belong necessarily to the peculiarly religious idea of God. Difficulties of the first kind became acute with that secularisation of the study of Scripture which has, after two centuries, assumed the dimensions of a vast and highly specialised intellectual discipline known to us as Biblical Criticism. The second type of difficulty, on the other hand, is as old as theology itself. Theology, indeed, had its origin in the attempt, never wholly successful and sometimes not even resolutely pursued, to reconcile these conflicting attributes. If, for instance, impassibility seemed to be a necessary attribute of the *Ens Realissimum*, and if, on the other hand, religion required that God should somehow suffer with His creatures, theology yielded unconditionally to the demands of Reason, asserted unreservedly even of the God of religion that He was *impassibilis*, and left the strictly religious requirements to the contrary to fend as best they might for themselves. Now, however, the pendulum has swung its full length in the opposite direction, and it is the metaphysical attribute that now remains almost fossilised in our religious formulas, while the religious postulate of a Suffering God is apparently dispensed from all need of accommodating itself to what was once an unquestioned position of every rational theology. It is hardly necessary to remind ourselves that this method of virtual cancellation of one of the refractory attributes, from whichever side it is used, leaves the original conflict entirely unresolved. A still greater difficulty, at least for the religious multitude, is the apparent conflict between the Divine attributes of Omnipotence and Justice presented by the existence of evil in the universe. Here, again, theology, in the person of its most influential Western exponent, came down definitely on the side of philosophy by giving a purely " privative " quality to evil, a solution which was again no solution because it has never satisfied the strictly religious conscience of Christendom, not even that of its originator himself. For St. Augustine as a thinker evil might be privative. But for the same St. Augustine as a religious soul it became the most positive thing in the world.

I have long been persuaded that these two types of difficulty are much more closely related than might at first sight appear. Though, therefore, my immediate purpose in these pages has been to determine what are the permanent and religiously essential elements in the traditional idea of Revelation, I have also cherished the hope of gaining by the way a clearer perception of the origin of the apparent conflict between the metaphysical and moral attributes of Deity, perhaps too of the conditions of their reconciliation.

The Christian religion has throughout its history hardly troubled to assert, so consistently has it taken it for granted, that it is in its entirety a revelation by God to men of His true nature and of His saving relations with them. When, however, it had to order and systematise the beliefs which had come to it with this peculiar kind of immediacy, it found that a necessary condition of doing so was a right use of the ordinary processes of discursive thinking and an accommodation of its own peculiar truths to a whole world of knowledge independently attained by the human reason. The intellectual discipline which sought to accomplish these ends was called theology. Theology has, in the course of its development, conceived of its task in very different ways. But it has never failed to insist that the contents of the Divine Revelation entrusted to it were the first principles of knowledge from which it started and to which it must return for the verification of every one of its conclusions. So long, however, as it was dominated mainly by Platonic influences and wherever such influences have been felt by it in later times, it may be said that revelation and reason became fused in a kind of theosophic amalgam which extended to the whole sphere of human knowledge. There were, indeed, characteristic differences even within the region of Platonic influence, of which Augustine, Scotus Erigena, and the mediæval Augustinians may be held to be representative. But with the coming of the Aristotelian influence there arose that type of theology which from the thoroughness of its methods, the majestic range of its systematisation, and the authority it imposed generally upon the religious mind of the West, even where that authority was afterwards challenged in detail, has a full right to recognition as the classical theology of Christendom.

It is the conception of Revelation and of its relation to ordinary knowledge which we owe to this theology that I have endeavoured to study in these pages. It may be said that it consisted in a determined effort to escape from the mere confusion of Revelation and Reason to which all Platonising theology tended. But the confusion inevitably crept in in another and not less disturbing fashion. The Platonic Reason was in the last resort a kind of divination, and therefore partook throughout of the nature of Revelation. Having pursued an elusive truth with all the pedestrian skill of its ordinary discursive methods, and pursued it thus unsuccessfully, it at last seized its flying skirts in the ecstasy of myth. For Aristotelian Thomism, on the other hand, reason needed no capital letter. Its achievements were as solid and secure as the earth on which it sought and found them. And when it followed truth into the region of Revelation it hoped to seize it there in the same net of precise definition in which it was accustomed to capture more mundane truth. In formal terms, indeed, it made abundant confession of the inadequacy of this instrument for receiving or conveying the truths of Revelation. But in practice it ignored this insufficiency. No truth which could not assume the dogmatic form, which had not in fact assumed it, was even in the field of Revelation worthy of being accounted a truth. And this, with all its consequences, is our actual theological heritage in the West.

Now the instinctive certainty of religion that the truth on which it is founded is simply given to it cannot, any more than any other instinctive certainty, be refuted by the reason. It is there for the reason to make the best of. Similarly the instinct of theology that it must accept the deliverances of Revelation as indispensable first principles of all its reasonings is an altogether sound one. There are here two positions as to the nature and import of Revelation which have a permanent value and with which religion will never permit any tampering. Yet it seems to me that theology in reducing the truth of Revelation to the cramped measure of exact dogmatic statement has in fact, however unconsciously, tampered with these positions. The truth given in Revelation is of an entirely different kind from the truth attained by the discursive reason. Not only is it never a conclusion but always an immediate certainty ; but it is also the immediate certainty of an object which impresses itself upon us so as to produce the most definite and intimate reactions in ourselves. It is primarily the kind of knowledge we gain of character through some intimate human relationship, but of a character so majestic and commanding that it stirs our own being to the depths and calls forth in it qualities and powers of which it had never before been fully aware. And as in the impact of such a character, but in a vastly intenser degree, another effect of this influence, which we instinctively feel and describe as personal, is to transform not only ourselves but our world of experience. The world in which, with our fellow-men, we had been the solitary actors now becomes a world directed by this Power to its own ends which seem to us a supreme and inclusive end of good. The God of religion commands, forbids, counsels, encourages, approves and condemns, rewards and punishes, and has, we feel deeply, and know because we thus feel, the sole right to do all these things. Things pass as before in time, but their record has become the record of the *Gesta Dei*. Even in their temporal succession they have taken on for us something of an eternal quality and have come to be of eternal moment. And having felt all this with a rapt immediacy which leaves no room for deliberate reflection, we express it also through the immediacy of passionate and gigantic symbol. Reflection will come later—and here theology has its birth—but it will come even then most fittingly and fruitfully as reflection which still continues to divine rather than pauses to analyse, as the Platonic reason rather than the Aristotelian logic.

Throughout the most rational moments of the acquisition of religious truth, therefore, its revelational quality still persists. It begins, continues, and ends as the divination of a personal knowledge. And yet, of course, the claims of pure reason in the realm of theology can never be denied. Here Plato may be taken perhaps as our most perfect model and most trustworthy guide. In the *Philebus*, for instance, the Platonic Socrates applies the severest form of dialectic to the discussion of the good, and more particularly of the sense which must be given to pleasure as an element in the good. The result of the discussion is, as might be expected, to refuse any share in the true good to the vulgar conception of pleasure. Yet the discussion opens upon the rapt mood of religious wonder. "My awe," he says, "in respect to the names of the gods is always beyond the greatest human fear." And it is of Aphrodite he is here speaking in that name of *Hedone* (Pleasure) "which is pleasing to her." The attributes of the gods which are disclosed in their very names are those from which reason, uplifted in mystic wonder, must begin its pursuit of truth about them. So, too, Plotinus, discussing the justice inherent in human destiny, the Karma of the soul, returns continually to "the divine formula Adrasteia, the Divine Name which expresses the true justice, the altogether admirable wisdom." And when reason has done its best to reconcile the primitive divinations of the religious sense with those fuller divinations of the nature of Deity which it has attained in its own laborious way, it is in the end compelled to seek that reconciliation, not in accurate formula, but in the free suggestion of poetic myth. Religion began in the primitive symbols which could alone express the immediate impressions of the Divine Power upon the individual soul. It ends in the inspired myths which interpret the vast tension of the universe as the outcome of a peace at its central heart, the Peace which passeth all understanding.

If therefore we are confronted, as we are and shall always continue to be, by conflicting elements in our conception of Deity, it is not by mere thinking from the outside that we can ever hope to reconcile them. It will rather be by the frank recognition of two complementary facts : the one that all the symbolism of Revelation, though the result of a process in which the reason has not consciously intervened, has nevertheless a fully rational character ; the other that every deliverance of the reason about the Divine Nature which has authentic religious value has been attained through a more than logical faculty of the intellect which can only be described as divination. He who holds firmly to these two positions will not quail before any antinomy which has arisen or can arise in our human conceptions of the Divine character. And he will probably shrink from the kind of dogmatic statement which virtually suppresses one of the terms of such an antinomy, and equally from the other kind which does no more than place them side by side in their bare unreconciledness.

NOTE

IT would be impossible for me to select even the principal texts on which I have relied for the account of St. Thomas's anthropology in Chapter II. Nor does it seem necessary, since the positions here set forth, however imperfect and fragmentary my exposition of them, belong to the general fabric of the great Doctor's thought and teaching. But it is otherwise with his special treatment of Revelation which is the subject of Chapters III and IV. It is usually incidentally upon the treatment of other themes, such as the nature of Theology or Sacred Science, Grace, and the relations between Theology and Philosophy, that this teaching occurs. It seems desirable, therefore, to mention the principal texts which I have used. They are:

i. *Summa Theologica*, First Part, Question i, Article 8, Reply to Second Objection, and the whole of Articles 9 and 10.

ii. *Contra Gentiles*, iii, 154.

iii. *The Seventh Quodlibet*, Question vi, Articles 1, 2, and 3 (numbered 14, 15, 16 in Mandonnet's edition).

iv. *De Potentia*, Question iv, Article 1.

The Opusculum numbered 39 in Mandonnet's edition, St. Thomas's first sermon as a Bachelor at Paris, is interesting as a popular exposition of the grounds of belief in the supreme authority of Holy Scripture during the mediæval period.

The study of Calvin's doctrine of Revelation in Chapter V, is based upon the relevant portions of the First Book of the *Institution de la Religion Chrétienne*.

SYNOPSIS OF CHAPTER I

M. Paul Valéry's statement of popular difficulties about belief in the Christian Revelation. His "problem of the priest." The Anglican theologian will be inclined to indict M. Valéry's statement of unfairness and unreality. M. Valéry's probable reply that such an attitude is an indictment, not of him, but of the uniform tradition of Christian theology solemnly reaffirmed in the Vatican Decrees of 1870.

M. Valéry justified in his contention. English theology of last two generations a noteworthy departure from traditional conceptions of Revelation. Stages in the change of view since J. B. Mozley's Bampton Lectures of 1865. Renewed insistence on an integral orthodoxy as alone fully Christian now widely prevalent among both adherents and opponents of Christianity, but not represented even in most conservative forms of English theology. This insistence most intelligible in view of fact that all Christian truth has rested hitherto on foundation of an infallible, inerrant, integral, insupersessible Divine Revelation.

Yet modification of traditional view rendered necessary by results of Biblical Criticism. Necessity accepted by English theology and even officially recognised at Lambeth Conference as serviceable to religion. Theory of a progressive revelation. Its difficulties. Revelation, Grace, Incarnation. Their connection and mutual support as manifestations of the necessary Divine priority in the work of human redemption. St. Thomas's doctrine of the "three contacts." His view of the Incarnation as "beyond reason" due to the logical contradiction involved in the doctrine. Co-existence of contradictory modes of being. English theology escapes the difficulty by concentrating on the moral attributes of God in which there is kinship between Divine and human, to a virtual disregard of the metaphysical attributes which deny of man everything affirmed of God. Thus humanistic note imported by English theology into its conceptions of Revelation, Grace, Incarnation.

I. THE STATEMENT OF THE PROBLEM

It was something quite accidental which led me to attempt the discussion of a problem, the urgency of which in the field of theology I have felt for many years. In the summer of 1930 I had been reading M. Paul Valéry's then latest volume of essays in literary criticism. In an appreciation of Stendhal, M. Valéry devoted some pages to a discussion which came to me as a personal challenge. When, a few months later, the invitation to deliver the Paddock Lectures reached me, the smart of that challenge was still there to determine my choice of subject.

M. Valéry calls attention to the fact that Stendhal rarely draws the portrait of a priest without leaving an impression of contempt and something like moral loathing. And the distinguished Academician thereupon turns aside to discuss at some length the justice of Stendhal's implied indictment of the priestly character. That indictment raises what M. Valéry calls the problem of the priest, or more accurately of the professional believer, which he admits at once is only a specialised form of the more general problem of the possibility of the believer in any kind.

Let me try to state the problem as nearly as possible in M. Valéry's own words. Let us assume, first of all, as in the case of the priest we are surely entitled to do, a man of instructed intelligence and wide general knowledge, one capable of observing and appraising fact without undue disturbance by vague desires and fears of his own of a temperamental and perhaps morbid character, capable, too, of distinguishing between the domains of fact and of fiction and of assigning to each its due value.   How is it possible that such a one can fail to reject to the realm of legend and fable all those narratives of bizarre and improbable events which are essential to the authority of every religion ? How can he fail to realise the fragility of the proofs and reasonings on which dogmas are founded ?   How can he fail to be astonished, to the point of refusing all credence to them, at finding revelations, that is, announcements of a literally infinite importance for man, offered to him in the form of Sphinx-like riddles which he must interpret at his peril, especially when these revelations are accompanied by such feeble guarantees of their truth, and are presented in forms so remote from those which he is accustomed to expect of things undoubtedly true ?   Is it possible to hold that the man who accepts such beliefs on such evidence can be at once intelligent and sincere ?   In other words, is it not impossible not to suspect either his intelligence or his sincerity ?   That is just what Stendhal does. For him the priest is necessarily either a fool or a hypocrite. M. Valéry, however, insists that the problem cannot be solved in this a priori fashion. The possibility of the believer who is both intelligent and sincere is for him a matter of experience. He has known many priests who were both by the whole tenor of their lives obviously sincere and at the same time endowed with intellectual powers of a high order. His experience has assured him of the fact. But he, too, has to admit that it is a fact which he cannot explain.

Now, I can hear the contemporary Anglican theologian impatiently brushing aside as wholly imaginary and unreal M. Valéry's statement of this problem. He will say perhaps that that statement implies a view of Scripture and of Revelation to which he feels himself in no way committed. He will even find himself empowered to reject the view thus implied on the authority of a committee of bishops of his own Communion, and to reject it, too, exactly in the interests of religion itself. He will, for instance, be able to point to a report of the recent Lambeth Conference which expressly ascribes certain inadequate and unworthy conceptions of God still current in the Church itself to the belief that all parts of the Bible have equal authority. Here, he will say, is at least indicated a view of the revelational character of Scripture which leaves our withers unwrung by M. Valéry's statement of his problem.

But M. Valéry, if the words of an English theologian ever reached his ears, would probably reply : " I was not when I wrote concerned with the eccentricities of English theology, of which for the rest I know nothing. I was thinking of the ancient and uniform tradition of Christian belief solemnly reaffirmed as recently as 1870 by the Fathers of the Vatican Council in the following terms : 'If anyone do not accept for sacred and canonical the whole and every part of the Books of Holy Scripture, or deny that they are divinely inspired, let him be anathema ! If anyone say that miracles cannot be, and therefore the accounts of them, even those in Holy Scripture, must be assigned a place among fables and myths, or that the divine origin of the Christian religion cannot be proved from them, let him be anathema! If anyone say that the doctrines of the Church can ever receive a sense in accordance with the progress of science other than that sense which the Church has understood and still understands, let him be anathema!' It is of this belief and all that it implies that I was thinking when I said that, though I know of a certainty out of my own experience that men of high intelligence do in all sincerity accept it, yet I cannot render to myself any sufficient account of such acceptance on their part."

Now, there are here two facts to which we cannot afford to shut our eyes. One is that M. Valéry is thoroughly justified in claiming that the belief which he finds it so inexplicable that any intelligent person of our own day can hold is the authoritative belief of traditional Christianity. And the other is that English theologians during the last fifty years have so gradually and almost imperceptibly drifted away from that belief, that there is hardly left among them to-day even one who would maintain it in the full measure of its ancient rigour. The extent of that drift is admirably suggested in a single sentence of a leading article in the London *Times* on the passing of Canon Newbolt. "Newbolt and his contemporaries," said *The Times*, "lived to see beliefs they held vital regarded as open questions even by extreme Anglo-Catholics, and the intellectual structure of the Oxford Movement no longer provides thoughtful people with an adequate refuge." So remote indeed has the traditional position become for most of us that it requires an effort, not only of memory, but of imagination, to recall the statement of it by J. B. Mozley in his Bampton Lectures of 1865, only five years before the promulgation of the Vatican decrees. The Christian religion is the divinely revealed truth contained in the Scriptures of the Old and New Testaments, divinely guaranteed by miracle and prophecy. No amount of internal evidence, Mozley contended, and contended with the consensus of eighteen centuries of Christian theology behind him, whether that evidence consisted in the natural adaptation of Christian doctrines to the deepest needs of the human heart, or in their fruits in a specific type of individual and social righteousness, could possibly guarantee the truth of Revelation, and that just because these internal attestations were rooted in rational reflection, whereas the very essence of a revelation was that it was beyond all discovery by the reason. Only miracle, therefore, and prophecy in its traditional acceptation as the clear and intentional prediction of future events, both of them beyond all range of merely human power, could guarantee the Divine character and therefore the Divine truth of a revelation.

I have thought it desirable that we should thus deliberately fix our attention on the immense distances traversed almost unconsciously by English theology in a little over two generations. Each stage of that Odyssey, indeed, *Essays and Reviews*, *Lux Mundi*, *Contentio Veritatis*, *Foundations*, *Essays Catholic and Critical*, has been marked by a cry of protest and alarmed recognition of a departure from ancient ways. But nothing has arrested the forward march. Even the most conservative forces among us have found themselves forced into taking up the torch and carrying it on another stage. But if this has been the course of events within the borders of the Anglican Communion, a very different tendency has, especially during the last ten years, declared itself outside those borders. The drift towards Rome which has in these late years become so marked a feature of the religious movement in Germany and Holland, and is only a little less marked in England and America, and the return to practising Catholicism of a growing number of intellectuals in France and Italy, both bear witness to an attitude very different from our own.

The Romeward drift in Protestantism may have many motives, but few competent observers will doubt that the motive which governs all others is the desire to submit to an authority which professes to guarantee the integral Christian tradition of the past. And the same desire is still more notably characteristic of the Catholic revival in France and Italy. The returning intellectuals in those countries will have no truck with any kind of modernism, with any reduction of the ancient faith as it was shaped intellectually by the mediæval schoolmen. And among those who wage war upon Christianity from outside the same tendency becomes more and more marked. They altogether refuse to recognise as Christianity anything less than the most rigorous form of the ancient orthodoxy. From Santayana down to Mr. Middleton Murry they all alike insist that the only Christianity of which an intellectual opponent can take account nowadays is the Christianity of Rome. And, to add to the general effect of this reaction, German Protestantism, under the leadership of Karl Barth and his disciples, is going back behind Schleiermacher and the whole modern trend in theology to the undiluted or rather intensified Augustinianism of Luther and Calvin.

I hope, therefore, I have been able to show that M. Valéry's type of criticism of the difficulties of Christian belief cannot lightly be dismissed as an ignorant misrepresentation. He is really dealing with what, up to our own day, has been the uniform tradition of the nature and credentials of Christian belief, with what again in our own day both friend and foe are labouring hard to represent as having an exclusive right to be such. It is just as well for us to realise that our own theological position is, to say the least, an unusual one, that the orbit we are pursuing round the sun of revealed truth may reasonably be regarded as somewhat erratic both by the orthodox traditionalist and by the alien critic of historical Christianity. The fact, indeed, has been abundantly recognised any time during the last thirty years by the interested observer whether within or outside our Communion. George Tyrrell used to say that Romanism and orthodox Protestantism were much nearer to each other than were Rome and what was then known as High Anglicanism. And quite recently two distinguished Anglo-Catholics, Mr. Milner-White and Mr. Wilfred Knox, have been proclaiming that the chief present function of the Anglican Communion is to take the lead in such modernising of Christian theology as is necessary if the Christian faith is to survive in a world of vast and deep-going intellectual change.

I need hardly say that such a task is a perilous one, and that until its success is finally demonstrated every step which it entails will be examined with a jealous suspicion.   It is quite right that it should be so, for the interests at stake are of a strictly infinite importance, and the difficulties in the way are almost incalculably great.   But our belief is that they must and can be surmounted.   And the first step towards surmounting them must be to take accurate account of what they are.   Now, I think it will be found that the most in-tractable of these difficulties centre round three main conceptions, revelation, grace, and incarnation, so closely related to one another that they cannot in fact be disjoined.   These three conceptions together con-stitute the fully revelational character of the Christian religion, of which Revelation in the narrower sense, the Revelation of Holy Scripture, has always been regarded as the key position.   Yet it is just that key position which we seem to have surrendered, if not in the beginning without a struggle, at any rate in the end without a qualm.   Let us again consider what Revela-tion meant throughout the whole past of Christendom, what it still means for the orthodoxy of the Roman schools.   It meant that the will of God for man's redemption and the manner of its accomplishment had been expressly revealed beforehand to man by God, that without that Revelation man could never have known anything of God's gracious purpose, that that Revelation was contained in the Scriptures of the Old and New Testaments and in certain oral traditions communicated by our Lord to His apostles, that this Revelation of Scripture and tradition was infallible and inerrant in all its parts, that to its original content nothing could ever be added nor from it anything be taken away, and, finally, that its revealed character was guaranteed by the prophetic form in which it was given and by the miracles which God wrought for that express purpose. That was the immemorial foundation of the whole pyramid of Christian truth, that infallible, inerrant, integral, insupersessible Divine Revelation.

Was it wonderful if Mr. Gladstone thundered against the blasphemous temerity of the critics in his *Impregnable Rock of Holy Scripture*, if Dr. Liddon shrank into his grave before the awful portent of *Lux Mundi*, if Dr. Mozley declared that he dared not believe the doctrines of the Incarnation or the Atonement on any grounds of reason, such as their consonance with the deepest needs and cravings of the human heart, or on any other ground than that they had been announced beforehand by God in a miraculously attested Revelation? Now, however, a Committee of the Bishops assembled at Lambeth declares, and is surely fully justified in declaring, that " in spite of the light long since thrown upon the conditions under which its several books were written and upon the progressive revelation of sacred knowledge they record, the Bible is even now too often treated as if every statement about God, contained in every part of it, must find a place in our present apprehension of Him." The most remarkable feature of that statement is its direct attribution of inadequate and unworthy conceptions of God to the continued maintenance of a view of the Bible on which all our forefathers in the faith had held that our only trustworthy knowledge of that faith depended.

But the question which is immediately more important for us is this—What theory of revelation are we to substitute for the traditional theory which they so clearly displace ? We should perhaps have been even more grateful to the Bishops for guidance towards a solution of this disturbing question than for the somewhat casual reminder that the traditional view has, at a very crucial point, viz. our knowledge of God, proved religiously insufficient and even misleading. But if they have not clearly stated a revised view of revelation, they have at least suggested one. Revelation has been in the past progressive, and apparently may continue to be so. For I find, in another part of the Report from which I have quoted, the following sentence : " We recognise that it is only through a passionate devotion to our Blessed Lord that men have advanced in their knowledge of His Nature and may hope to penetrate further into the mysteries of God." Now I happen to be one of those who share to the full this belief in the progressive character of revelation. But I have at the same time never failed to feel for myself the extreme difficulty, and for the Christian religion in its claim to universal recognition among men the hazardous nature, of the step from Revelation with a capital R to revelation with a small r.

What is the guarantee of this decapitalised revelation ? The answer which I find offered very generally to-day is—religious experience. The appeal is no longer, it is said, to authority, but to religious experience. But religious experience is determined by the framework within which it takes place. The religious experience of a Buddhist is necessarily different from that of a Christian. They resemble each other only in the fact that they are both experiences having the specific quality or character which we call religious. Or, to take a more modern instance, no reader, even the most unsympathetic, of Mr. Middleton Murry's confessions, in the book which he calls *God*, will be likely to deny that the experiences which he there describes are of the kind we call religious, that they are even akin in certain respects to those of the great mystics. Mr. Murry's experience, indeed, as he describes it, has a much greater right to the strictly revelational character than the experience of the ordinary Christian. For his account is of a something directly and individually given, whereas the ordinary Christian experience is mediated through an atmosphere of antecedent, well-defined, and highly social-ised belief. Yet no Christian will admit that Mr. Murry's belief, though thus apparently revealed, has any authority or indeed any kind of religious value for him. Granting, then, that revelation is progressive, there must be some Divine guarantee that every actual concrete stage of that progress is an authentic instance of Divine revelation.

This question of Revelation is, as I have said, at the very root of the claim of the Christian religion to universal empire over the souls of men. Its present

indeterminateness, an indeterminateness from which
there is no immediate prospect of escape, is our
greatest apologetic weakness. It is in the hope of
escaping that indeterminateness that so many now
take refuge in an authority which claims infallibility,
without scanning too closely its credentials to that
claim. But such a course is too clearly a counsel of
despair to remain for long a possible course for thinking men, however sincerely religious they may be.
Inspiration is a possible Divine activity in man. Infallible inspiration is not possible even for the Divine
omnipotence, because the creature thus inspired would
ipso facto have ceased to be man, would have become
something more, essentially other, than man. What
our Christian forbears wanted, by their doctrine of
Revelation, to do was to safeguard the saving truth as
directly revealed by God, just as by their doctrine of
grace they wished to assert the absolute sovereignty of
God's goodness over the human will. No truth
which did not directly issue without any kind of deflec-
tion from the Eternal and Perfect Truth was really,
completely, absolutely true. No goodness which was
not an effect of the omnipotent operation of the
Divine grace was really good. Nay, it was, however
materially good, in its essence sinful. But those
forbears of ours either ignored or took quite insufficient account of the fact that what God gave
was received by men, and that men in receiving
God's gifts, whether of truth or of grace, remained
men, creatures of most limited reach and imperfect
grasp, creatures, too, even at their best of a distorting
receptivity.

To us it seems no derogation from God's all-sovereignty that man, in receiving from the eternal source of his being those gifts, whether natural or supernatural, without which he could not be at all, still remains a very earthen vessel. To us truth and goodness are no less authentically God's free gifts because their growth to fruitage is determined by the very various nature of our human soil and climate. We do not want to be either mere naturalists or mere Pelagians. We think, indeed, we are neither, since we do verily believe that God is not only the Author but the Perfecter of every one of His good gifts, that He works in and with every soul that is sincerely seeking Him as the Perfect Goodness and the Perfect Truth. But we cannot shut our eyes to the very obvious fact, a fact of which the Incarnation itself is the perfect pledge and the supreme example, that God reveals Himself to men through their own natural and inescapable limitations.

Yet here again we may have to admit that the doctrine of the Incarnation helps us only because, even for the most orthodox of modern theologians, it has been almost unconsciously deflected in a naturalistic sense. We, of course, assert the Divinity of our Lord as uncompromisingly as ever, but we reach that assertion through a contemplation of the unique perfections of His humanity. We do not even shrink from the statement that our only adequate knowledge of God is attained through the Jesus of history. Even for those theologians who try to keep closest to the formal elements of the ancient theology, the influence of our fuller realisation of the reality and therefore the limitations of our Lord's humanity leaves its effect upon their conception of its relation to His Divinity.

If we would see how great is the change in this matter, let us consider the ancient teaching in its most highly rationalised form, let us take it in Aquinas' treatment of the Incarnation. There, on the very threshold of our quest, we are met by the fact that for St. Thomas there are two revealed doctrines, and in the strictest sense two only, which completely transcend human reason. Once, indeed, they have been accepted by faith as revealed, the reason can find distant analogies for them. But it can do no more. It cannot make them in the strict sense reasonable. Those two doctrines are the Trinity and the Incarnation. Yet the analogies which St. Thomas finds in the case of the Incarnation are so persuasive that to us it may at first sight seem strange that they should not have led him to regard belief in the Incarnation as altogether reasonable. St. Thomas distinguishes three modes of God's relations to His own created order. There is first His presence to that order in all the fulness of His essence and power, a presence in sole virtue of which that order continues or can continue to exist at all. If that presence were for one moment withdrawn from any least fragment of His creation, it would at once cease to be. Yet it is to be noted that this Divine *concursus*, as it is technically called, requires no consciousness of it, and therefore no conscious response, on the part of its beneficiaries. They passively receive that conserving Divine activity in virtue of which they are and continue in being. Above this *concursus* at the level of mere nature is God's gift of Himself in grace. Here

God so gives Himself that there cannot be mere passive acceptance of His gift. The gift of grace is of its very nature the awakening of full conscious response to all that God is for the soul. Through that response the soul becomes in a sense one with God, has an actual share in His nature of wisdom and goodness and love. But beyond the stage of grace God has condescended to another and infinitely higher mode of contact with created existence. He became one with it in the absolute fulness of being. There the reason is baffled utterly. The essentially illimitable and the essentially limited have become actually and indefeasibly one.

Now, St. Thomas distinguishes these three modes of God's contact with the created order in order to point their fundamental differences and so to prepare for the unique miracle of the third. But he also established a certain relation between them which has always seemed to me of peculiar significance for the apologetic rôle of Christian theology. He held that the Divine *concursus* in nature was a necessary condition of the Divine communion in grace, and that the Divine unity of innermost being with created existence which the Incarnation was would not have been possible without the antecedent contacts of both nature and grace. As grace was the fulfilment which nature itself demanded, so was the Incarnation the necessary fulfilment of both nature and grace. Yet in spite of this view of nature, grace, Incarnation as three ascending and complementary stages in God's relations to His creation, St. Thomas was none the less convinced that the Incarnation was a mystery for ever transcending the human reason. Why? Because for him the logical reason necessarily ruled the whole conception, and for the logical reason the very conception of the Incarnation was a flat contradiction. The Divine essence was one with the Divine attributes of omnipotence, omniscience, omnipresence, etc., and yet that essence had become one personal being with a human nature whose very essence was limitation in all these regards.

We, on the other hand, are sitting more and more loose to the metaphysical attributes of Divinity, and concern ourselves more and more with the moral attributes of a personal God. Those attributes have already the beginnings of a positive existence in man, from which he can ascend by an imagination rooted in feeling to the absolute of moral perfection in God. He is not condemned, as in the contemplation of the metaphysical attributes, to find in himself the mere unrelieved contradiction of the Divine. But we have gone farther still in our departure from traditional theology. The first stages of our indifference to metaphysics in theology were largely unconscious, an accident of our theological insularity, of the fact that the Reformation had cut us off from the scholastic tradition with a completeness which had no parallel in the case of Continental Lutheranism and Calvinism. But now we are beginning to abjure metaphysics in the interest of religion itself, to proclaim that God cannot be adequately known in terms of reason, but only in terms of the heart. That is no doubt a position which tends to enlarge religious conceptions into the freedom of poetic imagery instead of holding them fast to definite concepts of the discursive reasoning.

It may be a gain for the reality of personal religion. But I am afraid there is no hiding from ourselves the fact that it is an added difficulty for the apologetic which would aim at a universal validity. It will be my aim in the next three chapters to exhibit the measure of that difficulty by recalling the metaphysical tradition which we have so largely abandoned. In the fifth chapter I will attempt to estimate how far that tradition was modified by the sixteenth-century Reformers, while the last two will be reserved for a consideration of how we stand towards it to-day.

C

SYNOPSIS OF CHAPTER II

Christianity, Judaism, Islam founded on Divine Revelation. Formal differences do not affect fundamental agreement that without Revelation man could not have known adequately either his own true nature or God's saving action upon it.

Two stages in the doctrine of man's nature developed by Christian theology in the West, both directed to man's need of a Divine Revelation. Augustinian and Thomist. Man's imperfection traced by Augustine to the Fall. Man created with natural power to achieve his own blessedness. For Aquinas, on the contrary, man by nature an *ens incompletum*. If he had not fallen, he would still have needed grace, a special Divine assistance, to attain the Beatific Vision. Thus Thomist doctrine of man metaphysical as well as religious, the Augustinian religious only.

i. Limited nature of man's intelligence in the Thomist doctrine. Not intuitive like that of the angels, but confined to reasoning from sense-data. Such reasoning insufficient for attainment of the heavenly wisdom which Revelation alone can give.

ii. Thomist distinction of Nature and Grace established as two different modes of God's presence to man. By His natural presence God enables man's independent use of reason from which issues his ordinary knowledge (science). His supernatural presence needed to awaken full response, communion, with the Divine, and so to "elevate" the human mind to the higher wisdom.

Relation of Science to Revelation thus differently conceived of in Augustinian and Thomist traditions. Former tends to a confusion of the two, science being the study of the Divine *vestigia* in the created order, regarded as itself a minor revelation. Science and Revelation approach each other also because all man's knowledge is an immediate result of Divine illumination. In Thomism they are clearly distinguished both because the Divine Wisdom is beyond the reach of man's unaided powers, and because his ordinary knowledge (science) needs no special Divine illumination for its acquisition. Yet St. Thomas provides for a real and even intimate dependence of the supernatural upon the natural.

ledge of it. Only in a knowledge of the Divine
essence could it find its ultimate satisfaction. The perfected blessedness of the human soul consisted in the
intellectual vision of God. And though it could
never gain that vision *in statu viatoris*, yet all its earthly
pilgrimage could and ought to be a preparation for it.
And revelation and grace were the supernatural aids
to that preparation.

For an understanding of the rôle of these supernatural aids in the preparation of man for his spiritual
destiny it will be a help to consider the Thomist
anthropology from another angle. Every created
being is such in virtue of its participation in Divine
being. That, of course, is the very meaning of creation. Only God is self-subsistent being. Every
creature *is*, in every moment of its existence, by reason
of its participation in the Being which eternally is.
And that means that the original creative act of God is
one with the action of His Providence by which He
maintains in being His whole created order and every
least element in it. He is present in the wholeness of
His essence and power to every unit of His creation,
from a stone to an angel, in every moment of its existence. If that Presence were for a moment withdrawn
from the whole created order or from any fragment of
it, in that moment that wholeness or that fragment
would have disappeared into nothingness. But this
Presence has no other purpose than to preserve each
particular being in existence, to enable it to manifest in
action that particular aspect of being, that specific
nature, which is expressed in it. As being it is utterly
dependent. As nature it is endowed with a relative

independence. God's presence in and to nature is a bare *concursus*, asking for no response from it other than its own due functioning. Now man's specific nature is reason, and the Divine Presence to man in the purely natural order is the *concursus* which preserves his being in its natural functioning of reason. Man at that level has his rôle in the natural order. But the fullest performance of that rôle will never satisfy him. His reason itself desires a knowledge which it cannot reach *of* itself. It desires a communion with the ultimate Reality which from its side it can never even initiate. Yet man is sometimes aware of that communion. And in that awareness he becomes certain that that Reality has visited him in a new way, awakening response, making communion with it possible for him. It has revealed itself in the evocation of a hidden power in man which only its coming could have evoked. It is a theophany which requires and evokes recognition, a Divine utterance which waits for and obtains its answer. It is the Divine Presence in grace.

It was by means of this conception of the two orders of nature and grace, the natural and the supernatural, that Aquinas sought to do justice to the claims both of science and religion, of natural and revealed knowledge. Many have been repelled by what they regard as its bald schematism. Indeed, it is hardly an exaggeration to say that outside the Roman schools it no longer anywhere receives the serious attention it deserves. The fact must seem all the more strange when we remember that the specific occasion of the Thomist scheme was the challenge of a philosophy

entirely independent of Revelation, and its specific
purpose to justify the Christian Revelation as not only
consistent with the chief findings of that philosophy,
but as the completed wisdom to which it pointed yet
could not of itself attain. That, after all, is the task
which every theology has to face, in so far at least as
theology is something more than the apologetic of a
passing moment. The Christian thinker has not only
to find a place for theology in the whole system of
human knowledge, but must also demonstrate its right
to be regarded as the crown and completion of that
knowledge. It is his belief, a belief from which he can
never escape or seek to escape, that the truth with
which he is specially concerned is in some real sense
simply given, that it has not been and could not be
acquired by any mere process of reason. That it is
reasonable, and that its reasonableness can be demonstrated with more or less sufficiency, he also most
firmly believes. But that it is definitely revealed
knowledge is both the motive and the consentient
witness of all Christian faith. And the sole function
of theology is to demonstrate the reasonableness of
this faith.

Now the Augustinian tradition which persisted
throughout the twelfth and early thirteenth centuries,
from Anselm to Bonaventure, envisaged the task of
reconciling faith with reason in a very different fashion
from that which became general from Aquinas onwards. It may be said that its tendency was to treat
Revelation as a kind of revealed philosophy. The
whole content of revealed truth was capable of being
apprehended by the reason. The *credo ut intelligam* of

Anselm was simply the assertion that all that had been given to faith was so given that it might afterwards be known. The *credibile* and the *scibile* did not differ in their objective content, but only in the subjective method of apprehending that content. And knowing was a higher and fuller form of apprehension than believing. The apprehending value of belief was intermediate between that of mere opinion and that of fully rational knowledge. Even the greatest mysteries of Revelation, as, for instance, the triune nature of God, were apprehensible by reason apart from Revelation, as the instance of Plato proved. It is true that Hugh of St. Victor made a pointed exception of the doctrine of the Incarnation as a truth to which the human reason could never have attained without the help of Revelation. And it is the more interesting to recall this fact because so many modern theologians seem to regard the Incarnation as a doctrine which not only does no violence to the reason but of itself nullifies the bare distinction between the natural and the supernatural orders. Yet surely, unless we altogether ignore the metaphysical attributes of Deity, the instinct of the Middle Age on this matter was sound. That one and the same personal being can be at once illimitable and limited must ever remain a stumbling-block to the reason. The self-limitation of Deity is a truth which is possible for faith only.

For the Augustinians therefore, speaking generally, the human reason was capable of discovering independently all the truths of Revelation. What, then, was the value or even the need of Revelation? The first and most obvious answer was that, as the sufficient use of reason was the exclusive privilege of a few specially trained and specially gifted minds, Revelation was needed for the sake of the many who were not so trained or gifted. It affixed the seal of a Divine authority to truths which as the mere findings of human reason might have remained unknown or doubtful to the many. It proclaimed the necessity for all of a knowledge which, without it, would have been the intellectual appanage of the few. Even for those few it invested the accidental discoveries of reason with the sacred character of religious certainty. From every point of view belief in a truth as revealed was, if not absolutely indispensable, at least normally helpful, to its apprehension by the reason. The *credo ut intelligam* of Anselm and his Augustinian followers was the confession of an actual experience.

But there were other and more influential reasons for the Augustinian equation of the content of reason and faith. Both their conception of the natural order and their theory of knowledge inevitably led them to make this equation. For them the created order was itself a Divine revelation. It was throughout an expression of the creative ideas eternally existent in God. It existed in virtue of the Divine implantation of those ideas in it. They were the seeds, the seminal ideas, out of which its whole life emerged and grew to its fruition. The created order, therefore, was a dim and distant, but an authentic, revelation of the Divine perfections themselves, a vast symbolism of the eternal reality. And it was only as such a symbolism that the inheritors of the Augustinian tradition were interested in the study of nature. Their science was an imaginative quest of the Divine *vestigia*, the resemblances of the Divine attributes through which, as St. Bonaventure, last and greatest of the Augustinians, said, " God Himself shines forth in every creature." If, therefore, the mediæval Augustinians equated the knowledge-content of reason and faith, it was because they regarded the knowledge given by both as a revelation of the Divine nature.

But further, for them revelation was not only an objective character of the truth communicated. It was also a quality of the knowing subject. Reason was the effect of an immediate Divine illumination. It was only as illumined by the Sun of truth, to use Augustine's favourite phrase, that the mind could know at all. All its speculative reach and power were enabled by the shining upon it of the Divine Light. Hence the necessity, for the attainment of all real knowledge, of purity of soul. The mind which was wrapped in the obscuring mists of passion and prejudice could no longer see the truth save in perverse and distorted forms. This twofold character of Revelation as the revealing light and the truth revealed is exemplified, for instance, in such a work as Bonaventure's *Itinerarium Mentis in Deum*. That little mystical treatise is an exposition of the value of all knowledge from that of the technical arts up to the highest speculations of philosophy in the quest of the Divine wisdom. But it is also a reminder that each stage of the upward journey is and must be accompanied by a corresponding purification of the soul.

There are few more sudden and decisive breaches in the history of human thought than that which separated this whole mode of thinking from that which immediately replaced it. Its occasion was the discovery that nature was an independent realm of existence which deserved study for its own sake, which could be, and actually had been, thus studied. The translation of the Aristotelian Physics into the language of Western Christendom was no doubt only a recovery of long-buried knowledge, not a fresh discovery of the human intellect. But its effects were, on that account perhaps, the more immediately revolutionary. It is more difficult to resist the persuasiveness of a completed system than in the light of a new guess, however illuminating, to set about the construction of a new one. All that was necessary for the immediate acceptance of the Aristotelian exposition of the mystery of becoming was a mind capable of grasping its importance and conveying it to others. In the encyclopædic mind of Albert the Great the necessary instrument of popularisation was forthcoming. His still greater pupil St. Thomas with a marvellous divination saw at once the need, and in a brief lifetime himself accomplished the task, of adapting it to the Christian Revelation.

The main results of that revolutionary change may be briefly stated. The confusion between philosophy and theology came to an end. Philosophy, based on accurate observation of nature, was set free to pursue its task in the full measure of its capacity. Since, indeed, truth was all of a piece, there could be no ultimate conflict between the conclusions of philosophy and the deliverances of Revelation. And since there could be no appeal against the latter, it was obvious that the former must have been mistaken if they contradicted at any point the plain statements of Revelation. In that case reason was convicted of an illegitimate use of its own legitimate methods and had the warning it needed to trace the source and repair the nature of its error—a task which was well within its own competence. But the positive rôle and capacity of reason were unaffected by a control which was not so much limiting as corrective. Reason had its own laws and its own sphere of action and was not necessarily dependent on the illumination of a special spiritual discipline, as the Augustinians held. Even the accordance of its findings with the truths of Revelation depended on the due use of its own purely intellectual discipline. But it was fundamentally incapable of reaching the full measure of truth which man needed for his eternal blessedness. Only a special Divine Revelation could be equal to that end. The total effect therefore of the Thomist revolution was to establish the complete autonomy of the reason while at the same time securing for Revelation that definite uniqueness of character which the Augustinian tendency to treat it as a revealed philosophy had endangered.

But this schematic division of the spheres of Reason and Revelation might seem, too, to have its dangers which even the recognition of the necessary unity of all truth could not wholly avert. It was not, indeed, so much in the objective field of truth as in the subjective method of knowledge that the breach might appear insuperable. Reason was strictly confined to the data of sense. All the truth which it could ever hope to achieve was truth derivable from those data only. It was endowed with no special intuition which might enable it to transcend them. The *scibile* and the *credibile* might be one, but the *scire* and the *credere* were distinct acts. And however far the *scire* might reach, it still needed to be supplemented by the *credere*. The Augustinians, as we have seen, held that the whole content of Revelation was also knowable, even though the great majority of men might be incapable of such use of reason as would enable them to know it in fact. But for St. Thomas there were certain truths of Revelation, such as the Trinity and the Incarnation, which it was definitely beyond all power of reason to have discovered. They were and must always remain objects of belief, not of the fulness of knowledge. The utmost that reason could do was to discover certain analogies in its own field of knowledge which made their revealed truth more accessible to itself. Thus in virtue of the twofold manner in which truth comes to us, the kingdom of truth, even though one and single, is for us divided into distinct regions which we occupy under different terms of tenure. It is this separateness of tenure which Aquinas carries into the world of objective reality as the two orders of the natural and the supernatural.

The cleavage, if left here, might well seem, as it has in fact seemed to many, factitious and unreal. But much of this appearance of artificiality will disappear if we consider carefully the problem with which St. Thomas had to deal and his actual handling of it. For the Christian thinker the fact of Revelation has always to be honoured at its full face-value. For the mediæval Christian thinker that face-value was still more inescapable than it is for us. For him, speaking generally, there was no distinction between form and content, between the Divine message and its human reception. That distinction was not indeed altogether absent from the mind even of the mediæval theologian, as I hope to show in the next chapter. But it was at least reduced to a minimum. And whatever allowance was made for it, it remained that the Scriptures of the Old and New Testaments were throughout the very Word of God, that they had in their whole extent and in every part a full revelational value. In other words, their authority was absolute, could not at any point or in any degree be tampered with. The truth which they contained might be patient of different modes of interpretation, and these modes might correspond to a real hierarchical value and import, but it was all alike Divine truth. The literal meaning had not less revelational truth, though it might have less revelational value, than the highest anagogical meaning.

The truth of Revelation was therefore of an altogether different order from the truth of reason. And it was of a different order not only by reason of its origin but also by reason of its purpose. By nature man was a rational animal. And as every creature was endowed in its creation with a certain measure of independence through which it might express the creative idea which was its essence, man as a mere creature of nature expressed his essence in the use of his reason. But man did not belong only to the order of nature. In his created independence he had not

exhausted either the possibilities or the deepest needs
of his being. Those possibilities, those needs, could
only be satisfied by ascending out of and beyond the
measure of his created independence, the order of
nature, into the most intimate dependence of his spirit
upon the Eternal Spirit. That immediate dependence
was possible only through the self-revealing act of the
Eternal Spirit itself. The purpose of Revelation was
to admit man into the possession of that supernatural
order which he felt towards as the fulness of his
heritage, to complete the truncated being which was
his as a creature of nature only.

It was, then, an actual requirement of fact which
motived the Thomist conception of the two orders.
Man was in fact a creature of the nature whose function it was to manifest its essence in a relative independence of the Creator, and also a beneficiary of the
supernature in which the Divine Presence was so given
as both to enable and demand full spiritual response.
But St. Thomas did not conceive these two orders as
out of all relation to each other. In other words,
they were not so conceived by him that the one
remained simply natural and the other became simply
miraculous. The supernatural was not imposed on
the natural as something wholly alien to it, but required it as that without which it could not at all be
mediated to man. The order of grace completed the
order of nature by accommodating itself to it at every
point. If nature expressed itself in habit and discipline, grace was fitted into the same framework of disciplined habit. So, too, the knowledge given in
Revelation, in spite of its purely supernatural origin

D

and character, was dovetailed as it were into the knowledge acquired by reason alone. It seemed to solicit
the activity of reason for its more perfect understanding instead of simply over-riding it or ignoring altogether its aid. And, on the other hand, it acted as a
finger-post to reason pointing out the ways of its more
fruitful advance, or as a stimulus urging it to higher
and more generous activity. Thus nature and supernature, in spite of their schematic contrast, are in the
Thomist system woven together into the single
strand of the essentially human life.

It is difficult to see how the necessity of a Divine
revelation can be established apart from some such
doctrine of man as that which Aquinas bequeathed to
all subsequent Christian theology. Or perhaps it
would be more accurate to say that with any other
anthropology the rôle and character of Revelation
become somehow different. For Augustine, who
conceived of the Fall as the total corruption of a
nature originally perfect and complete, Revelation
needed to be nothing more than the proclamation and
manifestation of the Divine action by which the recovery of that original perfection was made possible.
Aquinas by his very definition of nature, a definition
which accorded with the scientific realism of rational
knowledge, found man as a creature of nature incom-
plete. If he had never fallen he would still have
needed for the blessedness to which his nature tended
a knowledge which that nature with its reason
tethered to the things of sense could never of itself
have attained. Since he needed that knowledge, he
needed also that it should be simply given. And that

knowledge was more than the means of recovery from his fallen state. It was the disclosure of the secrets of the eternal order, the unveiling of the mystery from which he had come and to which he would fain return. The degree in which that unveiling was at all possible must be the subject of another chapter.

SYNOPSIS OF CHAPTER III

Revelation a real enabling or " elevation " of the mind to know the truth revealed. Error of Montanus and Priscilla. Touchstone of genuine inspiration the heightening, not the supersession, of intelligence. Thus all mere separation between natural and supernatural in revelation avoided.

God's revealing activity not confined to enlightenment of original medium of Revelation. Some measure of Divine assistance necessary to (1) its translation into human language, (2) its transmission, (3) its interpretation, (4) its initial appropriation by faith (*fides informis*), (5) its perfected appropriation by the will informed by charity (*fides formata*), in order that it might be a Divine act throughout. Thus Revelation in a real sense the totality of the economy of grace.

Twofold accommodation of Revelation to man's imperfection : (1) to the imperfection of human intelligence, (2) to the imperfection of human language. The knowledge it gives such only as man needs and is capable of receiving *in via*. And it is given necessarily in images drawn from the world of sense. The Incarnation, or God hidden in humanity, the norm of all Revelation. Bossuet's " simplicity of the letter " the Divine Seal set upon the Sacred Scriptures. St. Thomas's insistence on the sacredness of the letter as the chosen vehicle of the Spirit for the communication to man of the truth he needed. *Salvâ literae circumstantiâ.*

St. Thomas's method of discussing difficulties in interpretation of Scripture. Such discussion may be conducted either as (1) a question of pure philosophy or (2) as a question of Biblical exegesis. Two dangers attend the first method : (1) that of asserting any position incapable of accommodation to the widest meaning of the letter, and (2) the assumption that every interpretation of the letter which *seems* true is necessarily of the content of faith. The purely exegetic method also attended by two dangers : (1) that of asserting anything to be the teaching of Holy Scripture which the reason plainly declares false, and (2) that of denying that a Scriptural text may be capable of different interpretations. His criterion of the legitimacy of various interpretations.

III. THE METHOD OF REVELATION

It is well to remind ourselves at every stage of our progress that the specific function of Christian theology is to explain, or at least to render a reasonable account of, the constitutive character of the Christian Religion as faith in a Divine Revelation. The primary task of theology, therefore, was to demonstrate man's need of Revelation. That need could be established only if man were shown to be unable of himself to acquire the kind or degree of knowledge which was indispensable for the perfecting of his own nature. Such incapacity might be traced to the self-betrayal of human nature by the Fall, which, however, as itself a datum of Revelation, was from the standpoint of pure reason invalidated as evidence of an original capacity. The theory of Aquinas, however artificial it might seem, had at least the advantage of avoiding all prior resort to Revelation. Besides, the appearance of artificiality in the Thomist system was considerably reduced, if not altogether eliminated, by the intimate dependence of the supernatural upon the natural which it predicated. If the rational nature of man could not of itself attain to a fully saving knowledge of God, it had at least a natural desire of such knowledge. Revelation, though a free gift of God, a *gratia gratis data*, was yet the satisfaction of man's actual need on the plane of mere nature.

But this intimate connection of the natural and the supernatural appeared still more fully in the method of revelation as expounded by Aquinas with minutest care. In the first place, it was only by a special illumination of the mind that God could reveal or ever had revealed any truth to man. The error of Montanus and Priscilla was that they believed that prophets were so possessed by the Spirit as not themselves to understand their own inspired utterances. The touchstone of genuine spiritual possession was a heightening of intelligence, not its supersession. The truth which the reason could not of itself attain it must yet with the aid of the Divine illumination clearly recognise as truth. The result of revelation was an intellectual certitude, and it was so because revelation itself was an inner intellectual light enabling the mind to perceive realities denied to its own unaided vision. The mode of revelation might vary. It might be an actual audition or vision, an actual word formed by the Divine power and heard as such by the human ear, or some corporeal appearance produced by that same power and seen by the human eye. Or, again, it might be an inner word or vision, the co-operation of the Divine power with man's image-making faculty or rather the Divine use of that faculty to communicate truth. But neither outer nor inner audition or vision was sufficient of itself to communicate the Divine truth. It was apprehended only in virtue of the inner light which heightened the actual powers of the mind. And that inner light was sufficient of itself, without any adventitious aid of things seen or heard whether outwardly or inwardly, to perceive the truth revealed.

St. Thomas, therefore, in his doctrine of revelation carefully refrained from any and every position which might lead to a vital separation between the natural and supernatural orders. By mere reason, indeed, of his conception of revelation as the necessary satisfaction of man's highest need it was impossible that he should do so. But, on the other hand, he did not think of the supernatural as simply given to the natural to use henceforth as it might. The whole religious life of man was a continuous action of the supernatural upon the natural, eliciting those possibilities of which it had a dim awareness, yet could never of itself have made actual. Let us see, then, how this continuous interaction of the natural and the supernatural is illustrated in the further development of the Thomist doctrine of revelation. And it may be well here to remind ourselves once again that for St. Thomas the supernatural is simply the Divine action awakening full conscious response in that on which it acts, while the natural is the relatively independent activity of which every created being is capable in virtue of its particular mode of being.

We have seen, then, how revelation is given through a Divine illumination which " elevates," to use St. Thomas's own language, the mind to a perception of truths of the invisible order which are necessarily beyond its own reach as limited by the sensible order through which alone it operates by nature. But the revelation was not given for the sake only of those who originally received it. It was given to them only that they might communicate it to all others whom they could reach, who in turn should communicate

it to others until it became known to all mankind.
It might seem that this at least was a work which
man could accomplish in virtue of his own unaided
nature. But a moment's reflection will convince us
that this is not at all the case. No revelation of God
can be simply handed on by man. In every instance
of its reception the same kind of Divine illumination
which first made it a revelation is required. It does
not become less a revelation because spoken by human
lips or heard by human ears. The faith by which
alone it can be received is also an immediate gift of
God, a *gratia gratis data*. Revelation is always and in
each particular instance transmitted from faith to
faith, from a Divine act to a Divine act, whatever the
human medium may be. In the Divine economy of
revelation man can never be more than an instrument
of the Divine purpose, and at best, too, an *instrumentum
separatum*. Only in the Incarnation did man become
an *instrumentum conjunctum* of the Divine will, an instrument organically united with it as a man's arm, for
instance, is the instrument of his will.

But even though faith as an adhesion of the mind
to revealed truth is a gift of grace, it yet reasonably
asks for guarantees that the truth to which it adheres
is really of God. These guarantees, therefore, must
themselves bear the unmistakable Divine signature.
That all legitimate doubt as to the revealed character
of that which claims to be a revelation may be removed,
it must be accompanied in those who originally received and transmitted it by gifts of power whose
origin was unmistakably Divine. Such were the gifts
of miracles and prophecy bestowed upon those who

were sent forth to proclaim the original Gospel. When our Lord commissioned the disciples to preach the Gospel of the imminence of the Kingdom of Heaven, He empowered them also to heal the sick, cleanse the lepers, raise the dead, cast out devils. For Aquinas and his age these works were all on the same miraculous level. They witnessed to a power which was immediately of God and were themselves the sufficient witness that the truth proclaimed by those who were empowered to work them was of God. So, too, the gift of prophecy, whether in the sense of foreseeing and foretelling future events or in that of reading the secret thoughts and desires of others, was manifest evidence of the Divine illumination of him who possessed it. In the " signs following " God set His authentic seal upon His revelation, distinguishing it convincingly for faith from all spurious claimants to that character.

But Revelation as a Divine gift to mankind had also to enter into history. And that it might be saved from becoming a mere thing of history, it needed here once again a continuous Divine protection. The imperfection of human language was but the first of the hampering conditions from which the integrity of the revealed truth had to be defended. Even when committed to a fixed written form there was the continual risk of misinterpretation. At every point a special Divine grace was present to preserve the fully revelational character of the truth originally revealed. The labour of patristic interpretation was invested with authority only because believed to be conducted throughout with a protective Divine assistance. The duty of the Christian preacher, again, was a sacred responsibility which depended for its due discharge upon the sincere and disciplined desire of that same assistance. Throughout all the accidents of history Revelation was thus preserved by the continuous action of that Divine grace through which it was originally given.

But this merely objective preservation of revealed truth was nothing more than a protective preparation for its due use. Only in its actual appropriation by human souls was it fully and worthily preserved. And here grace took on a new character. Faith as the initial act of that appropriation was possible only through Divine assistance. The most fatal virus of the Pelagian heresy was its assertion that man was of his own natural power capable of making an act of faith in Divine Revelation, that he could of himself believe what of himself he could never have known. But even faith was only preparatory. It was nothing more than the acceptance as true, and as Divine truth, of that which had been revealed. Yet in being such an acceptance it had in it the seeds of the whole supernatural life. For that which was revealed to it was the secret of man's deepest need, of his innermost desire, a need and a desire which on the plane of mere nature continually eluded him. Through Revelation not only the true nature and urgency of his own need was made manifest to man, but also the true nature of its satisfaction. And the faith by which he merely accepted Revelation as the only sufficient guide to the end for which he was made was at least a beginning of his supernatural life. By the grace of faith he at least knew on Divine authority the nature of that life in tion " of the mind which would be able to receive it, in the extraordinary powers which accompanied those to whom its original transmission was entrusted, in the faithful long-continued labour of its right interpretation, in the faith which accepted it, in the love which fully embraced it, the Divine act was always beforehand. From the purely logical point of view it was always possible, from that point of view it might be also convenient, to distinguish Revelation as but a single moment in the economy of grace. But from the wider, and the only religiously satisfying, point of view it was that economy in its totality. Only by giving it this width of range and actuality could it be equal to the needs of man as a creature of the supernatural order. Man as a creature of mere nature could never have ascended into that order which yet he could never cease to desire. It had to descend to him to fulfil his desire, to draw him upwards into itself in the power of a fully enabled will.

Yet St. Thomas was far too much of a religious realist to forget for a moment the limitations of human capacity, and too deeply sensible of what religion as the reality of the bond between man and God required, to conceive of God as forcibly removing those limitations. Revelation, therefore, was not, because it could not be for man, the gift of a perfected knowledge of the invisible world. It did not and could not, because man was man, give the knowledge of the Divine essence, of the reality of the Divine nature as known to itself. In Revelation God is not only speaking to man but is speaking also to all sorts and conditions of men, to the rude and unlettered as well as to those who are capable of the highest degrees of intelligence possible for man. Now the human intelligence at its highest is incapable of that immediate vision which is the peculiar privilege of the separated (*i.e.* immaterial) substances, such as Aquinas conceived the angels to be. Revelation, therefore, was not the communication of a knowledge which man was incapable of receiving, the immediate vision of the Divine reality. Even when divinely inspired, the human mind received Divine truth *per speculum*, through distant images only. And those mental images had in turn to be translated into human speech. Hence the prevalently metaphorical character of the revealed Word as transmitted in its written form to men.

Aquinas took full account of this twofold accommodation of the Divine thought in its transmission to man, its accommodation to the imperfection of the human intelligence and again its accommodation to the imperfection of human language. He accepts this necessary refraction of revealed truth due to the human medium which receives it so frankly as to make it clear that he finds in it no inconsistency with that Divine guidance in every moment of its transmission which he had already predicated as essential to its revelational character. He asserts, indeed, with St. Augustine that the difficulties which beset the correct interpretation of Holy Scripture are a proof of its Divine origin. They witness to the useful provision of the Divine wisdom that the truth which it gives should not lull the mind into an ignoble rest but stir it on to a healthy and vigorous activity. "It is just the things that are difficult that make the mind eagerly learned, that was regarded as the unmistakable Divine seal set upon the Sacred Writings. The literal meaning of Scripture had a peculiar sacredness of its own which must never be tampered with. It was the chosen vehicle of the Holy Spirit for communicating to man the measure of Divine truth which he needed. That fact alone was its title to an unbounded reverence. Theology, indeed, as the science, the ordered knowledge, of Revelation had laid upon it the duty of searching for the further and deeper meanings which often underlay the letter, to which the letter pointed on. But those meanings were always subject to the final control of the letter in which the Spirit had directly spoken. St. Thomas, of course, as a theologian was continually engaged in seeking himself such legitimate inferences from the text of Scripture, or in discussing the legitimacy of the inferences of others. But in doing so there is no phrase which is more continually on his lips than this—*salvâ literae circumstantiâ*. No interpretation can be regarded as acceptable which is clearly inconsistent with the plain content of the letter.

Let us take as an illustration of his theological method his discussion of the question whether the creation of formless matter preceded in time the creation of things. It is contained in the first Article of the Fourth Question of the *De Potentiâ*. The question is whether or not there was a time-interval between the creation of formless matter and the creation of things in their actual nature. For the Christian philosopher the answer to the question is necessarily controlled by the statement of Revelation. " In the

E

beginning God created the heaven and the earth ; and the earth was without form and void." What is the meaning of formlessness here ? Some have held that it is the formlessness of *prima materia*, of matter as the merely potential and as yet entirely undifferentiated substrate of all the actual variety of being *in rerum naturâ*. If so, there is no need to posit any lapse of time between the creation of matter and of things in their actual form and nature. The interval between them is logical only, not temporal. This is the opinion of Augustine, and is evidently in complete accord with the statement of Revelation. But others have maintained that the word " formless " is here used to indicate a stage of incompletedness in the formation of nature which admits of and, indeed, requires an actual time-interval for its due completion. In that case the Creator brought things *ex nihilo* into an imperfect state of being before, in a definitely temporal sense, constituting them in the ultimate perfection of their nature. This was the opinion of Basil, Gregory, and others, and is clearly not in conflict with the revealed word, since on the one hand it refutes the heresy which would limit God's creative act by positing the formation of the world out of an uncreated matter, and on the other provides for His sole activity in creation against those who would ascribe to other causes the formation of the lower grades of being. The *circumstantia literae*, therefore, St. Thomas concludes, is patient of both interpretations.

But I have instanced this discussion less for its own intrinsic merits than for the general rules which Aquinas lays down as governing all such discussions for the Christian thinker. A question of this kind may be discussed in one of two ways. It may be approached as a question of pure philosophy or as a question of Biblical exegesis. In the first case, the immediate matter of discussion is the truth of things as accessible to the reason, in the second the meaning of the letter of Scripture which contains that same truth as divinely revealed. Now, if the first method be adopted, there are two dangers in the way against which the inquirer after truth must be constantly on his guard. He must be careful not to be betrayed into the assertion of any position which is utterly incapable of accommodation to the *literae circumstantia*. For such a position must be simply false. But, on the other hand, he must not forthwith assume that an interpretation of the Scriptural letter which seems true to him must be necessarily of the content of faith, and therefore immediately applicable as a criterion of the findings of reason. If, however, the exegetical method of discussion be adopted, there are equally two positions to be avoided. The first is that of asserting anything which is plainly declared false in the court of reason as the teaching of Holy Scripture. For Scripture cannot teach anything which is false, and therefore cannot mean to teach as true that which the reason legitimately denies. The second is the denial, whether implicit or explicit, that Scripture may have more than one meaning. That is a fatal error for the sufficient exposition of Scripture. Scripture, Aquinas quite definitely holds, has many senses. He even ventures the opinion (*non est incredibile*) that Moses and the other authors of Holy Scripture were divinely permitted to know these different senses and embraced them all in the single literal form which they adopted (*in una serie literae*), so that each of them was a true sense for its author. On the other hand, there may be truths which the author did not know, and yet which, known to later expositors as deliverances of the reason, have been by them accommodated to the letter of Scripture. These truths were without doubt in the mind of the Holy Spirit as the original author of Holy Scripture. St. Thomas concludes that every truth which can be adapted to Scripture without injury to the content of its letter has a just right to be regarded as its meaning. *Omnis veritas quae, salvâ literae circumstantiâ, potest Divinae Scripturae aptari, est ejus sensus.*

In the next chapter I shall have to speak more fully of the importance attached by Aquinas to the manifold-ness of the sense of Scripture. What I have been anxious to show here and now is rather the capital rôle which he assigned to the letter itself as *the* heavenly, and not a mere earthly, vessel expressly formed to hold the manifold fulness of its divine content. The orthodox tradition of reverence for the letter has had no more uncompromising defender than St. Thomas, even when he applied that tradition with an intelligent freedom which few of his successors could emulate or even seemed desirous of emulating.

SYNOPSIS OF CHAPTER IV

Old Testament a Revelation mainly through events. The *Gesta Dei per Hebraeos*. The mediæval mind sought meaning and explanation of history not in the inner connection and independent motivation of its events, but in a purpose outside and beyond of which its events were occasional instruments. Symbolical interpretation of much in Scripture and especially in Old Testament, therefore, necessary.

Manifoldness of meaning in certain Scriptural texts justified by difference between human ideas and Divine ideas. The former, and therefore the words in which they are expressed, represent things. The latter created things to represent the higher Realities eternally existent in the Divine ideas themselves. In Scripture, therefore, as the Word of God, the things represented by its words represent also other things belonging to a higher order of reality.

St. Thomas's classification of meanings of Scripture : (1) literal or historical, (2) allegorical, (3) moral or tropological, and (4) anagogical, designed to correspond with these grades of reality. Comparison with that of Augustine which Thomas rejects as insufficient. Literal or historical meaning conveying plain sense of Scripture distinguished from other three which are all alike *spiritual* as embracing the further meanings contained in the letter.

The allegorical meaning represents first grade of higher reality pointed to by the letter. Thus all that is said of the Synagogue in the Old Testament has its literal value in its account of the Divine dealings with and promises to Israel, but is also an allegory of the Church in which those promises were fulfilled. Necessity here of careful distinction between allegory and what is merely metaphor.

The moral and anagogical meanings represent a still higher grade of reality than the allegorical, and are distinguished from each other by the kind of reality with which each deals. Divine teaching is either (1) of things to be done, or (2) things to be believed by man. The moral sense of Scripture conveyed, *e.g.*, in the Divine Life of Christ considered as exemplar of the way of man's communion with God. The anagogical, in what is said in Scripture of the Divine Life and of the Church on earth considered as symbols of the heavenly realities to which they point.

IV. THE INTERPRETATION OF SCRIPTURE

Some thirty years ago, when travelling in Bosnia, I was talking one day with a young Turkish official of the Austrian administration, who had had a Western education, about the possibilities of progress in the Moslem world. When I pressed him for his reasons for a too evident pessimism, he answered without a moment's hesitation, " Our people have no sense of history." I felt that that answer had revealed in a lightning flash the depth of the abyss which separated East from West, and in spite of superficial appearances will separate them for generations to come. The same gulf yawns, and to unsuspected depths, in the West itself between the modern and the mediæval ages. A historical commission appointed to delimit their frontiers might draw, would indeed be forced to draw, a very hesitant and wavering line across the surface of history. But surface frontiers mean little where there is question of a fundamental change in human outlook. The modern world began with the possession of the human mind by the sense of history. The mediæval did not need even to possess it. The modern world looks with eager curiosity before and after, where the mediæval looked with a torturing anxiety within and beyond.

Nowhere has this revolutionary change left a deeper impress than in the sphere of theology as the science of

Revelation. Revelation was regarded by the Middle Age, as it is no doubt still regarded by us, as the first principles of the knowledge of God. But it was the function of theology to elicit and systematically arrange the whole sum of truth which lay implicit in those *principia*. Everything depended upon the right interpretation of Scripture. Now interpretation must depend largely upon method. And there is no aspect of mediæval theology which is so strange and baffling to us as its method of Scriptural interpretation. Yet, just because theology is rightly the most traditional and conservative of sciences, many of the results of a method which seems to us merely bizarre are deeply imbedded in theological positions which we never think of questioning. There is of course no reason why this should not be so. Truth is greater than the explicit reasons which are used to justify it. But the fact that we hold the same truth on other grounds does not absolve us from the duty of paying due attention to a method of interpretation which was once universal and is as yet far from being universally abandoned.

Before, however, attempting a survey of this field it is necessary to deal with an objection which may fairly be urged against all that I have been saying. It may be admitted, I hear the objector intervene, that the sense of history has since the time of Niebuhr developed with an intensiveness and on a scale which may justly be described as revolutionary. But after all, some sense of history did exist before. The great Greek historians were at least pioneers in the study, and a highly intelligent and even critical study, of human events for their own sake. And they had Latin imitators who rank only just behind them, if indeed we ought not to place Tacitus and Thucydides on the same level. Then, too, within the distinctively Christian pale my friend and colleague Canon Streeter has made out a good case for admitting Eusebius to the ranks of the really critical historians. It is surely hardly credible that such masterpieces, even if of a still primitive type, could have been produced in an entirely unresponsive atmosphere. At least in the little Greek states and in the Roman Imperium which absorbed them there must have existed that valuation of the dramatic movement of events in time which has a right to be called the sense of history. And if this is admitted, as it surely must be, can we deny to Israel, so religiously preserving the record of its own past, a share in that sense, especially when we remember how impersonal its record is, the crystallised memory-deposit of the soul of a people rather than a product of the conscious artifice of professional historians? Surely we might rather say that it was just the sense of history which the Divine Author of Revelation had chosen as His special human medium.

Now, very much of this I could say as heartily as my objector. Indeed, I may confess that I have said it quite deliberately in my own name. Yet I would claim the right at almost every point to use a scholastic ' *distinguo*.' All peoples at all times are no doubt impressed by the passing show of things. But the question is, how are they impressed by it? Is it a tale told by an idiot, full of sound and fury but signifying ultimately nothing? Or is it the authentic fabric of reality, woven patiently on the loom of time?

These, indeed, may be regarded as representing ideal
limits of valuation rather than actual measures which
have ever been rigorously applied.   But it can hardly
be denied that the East has always approached very
closely to the one limit while the distinctively modern
world alone approaches the other, though it may be
admitted that the Greeks were also distantly attracted
towards it.   The Jews, however, and the mediæval
Christian world, it seems to me, found refuge in an
intermediate attitude.   The reality of history was to
be found in the purposes of God wrought out through
the deeds of men.   And not all the deeds of men had
this high value.   Most of them, indeed, were just un-
regarded happenings which left not a trace behind,
while those which did possess this value were not so
much the deeds of men as the deeds of God using man
as His instrument.   The history of Israel was the *Gesta
Dei per Hebraeos*.   The history of the Frankish tribes
which established their sovereignty over Roman Gaul
was, for Gregory of Tours, the *Gesta Dei per Francos*.

Now, since a very large portion of the Old Testament consisted of the history of Israel thus conceived,
it was quite true that God had chosen to reveal Himself largely through events, through actual happenings
in time.   And for the Middle Age, which we must
remember shaped all our theology, this was a real
stumbling-block, a stumbling-block which was removed by its peculiar method of interpretation.   We
may therefore now proceed to inquire what that
method was.   As we saw in the last chapter, the
literal sense of Scripture had the right to supreme
control over all other senses which might be legiti-

mately given to it. It alone was immediately and fully intended by its Divine Author. And it would be found, the mediæval expositors held, that wherever the literal meaning seemed to be obscure or even impossible of acceptance as the real expression of the Divine mind, some other portion of Scripture removed the obscurity or the offence.

Thus Holy Scripture, if only studied with sufficient care, was always of itself a sufficient guide in the elucidation of its own difficulties. But even though God had set the seal of His own authority upon the letter, it did not follow that the obvious sense of the letter exhausted the whole of the meaning which He intended. For men words represent things. That is their sole purpose. In their designation of things their total significance is exhausted. But the Divine mind is not so limited. For it things are the symbols of other things. The creative Word did not express itself in words but in things. Every created thing is the expression of a creative idea. Now one of God's gracious purposes in Revelation is to admit us to the fullest knowledge of those creative ideas which it is possible for us as creatures of time to possess. Scripture therefore is meant to lead us not only into a knowledge of the things which its words represent, but also still further into a knowledge of the Divine realities which those things represent. Scripture is of itself a discipline in the intelligence of the symbolism of the created order, and that discipline is independently required for its due understanding. It was only, indeed, for the sake of its spiritual symbolism that theologians of the Augustinian tradition thought nature worth studying. If Aquinas had advanced to the conception of an independent value in the study of nature, he had not on that account cut himself loose from the tradition of symbolism. Natural things for him still signified, or could signify, spiritual realities.

There are, then, many senses in the sayings of Scripture, and it is the duty of the expositor to exhibit these various meanings. Yet it must be remembered that not every Scripture saying has this manifold of meaning. For many of its sayings the wholeness of meaning is exhausted in the obvious sense of the letter. And again every merely arbitrary exposition was an offence against the Divine dignity of Scripture. All exposition other than the literal must, as I have said already, be controlled by the truth as plainly revealed in the letter of some other passage. Hence the paramount value, for the expositor, of theology as the systematic collation of revealed truth. Only as theologian was he likely to be capable of correct exposition. But as trained expositor he might always add to the richness and fulness of theological knowledge. In the Middle Age the field of theology was not yet closed; the work of the theologian, however anxiously respectful of traditional authority, was still freely and even boldly speculative.

The actual classification of the various meanings of Scripture which Aquinas adopted and which from his time onwards became traditional was fourfold, the literal or historical, the allegorical, the tropological or moral, and the anagogical. The classification itself, indeed, is due to the Venerable Bede. But it was St. Thomas who gave to it a really scientific motivation and value. And it is therefore as conceived and used by him that it calls for our careful attention. The principle which underlies it is the broad distinction between the literal meaning and the others as all of them alike spiritual. The importance of this principle in St. Thomas's eyes will be apparent from his criticism of St. Augustine's division, which is also fourfold. St. Augustine, in the *De utilitate credendi*, had distinguished between the historical, the ætiological, the analogical, and the allegorical senses to be found in Scripture. But St. Thomas points out that this method of division has little scientific value for theology, seeing that the first three belong all alike to the letter, while only the fourth, the allegorical, is reserved for the spiritual meanings whose distinctiveness of import and value cannot be reduced under one kind only. For St. Augustine the historical meaning is given in every plain, literal statement of Scripture. But he then goes on to distinguish from this sense something which is really well within the *circumstantia literae* and not merely a legitimate extension of its interpretation, viz. the reason assigned for some particular saying, as when our Lord explains that the reason why Moses commanded the Jews under certain circumstances to put away their wives was because of the hardness of their hearts. This assignment of a reason Augustine distinguishes in a class of its own, the ætiological.

It may be interesting here to instance, as an example of the naïve realism which is characteristic of so much mediæval interpretation, St. Thomas's own explanation of ' because of the hardness of your hearts.' What, Aquinas very naturally asks himself, could be the

hardness of heart which induced Moses to give permission, which *ex hypothesi* is Divine permission, for
divorce ?   It is, he says quite simply, that the Jews
were addicted to the bad habit of killing their wives,
quia scilicet proni erant ad occisionem uxorum, and therefore God permitted the lesser evil of divorce to prevent
the greater evil of murder.   I think we can hear there
an echo of contemporary Christian conceptions of life
in the Ghetto *re*jected into the history of two thousand
years before.

But to return to St. Augustine, by analogy he
meant merely the comparison of one literal text with
another with a view to showing that there is no repug-
nance between them.   All these three distinctions of
Augustine's, therefore, are distinctions within the plain
content of the letter.   Hugh of St. Victor, on the other
hand, had not offended so deeply against the requirements of an adequate classification when he defined
the various meanings of Scripture as the historical, the
allegorical, and the tropological.   Here there is no
confusion consequent on an unnecessary splitting up
of what is immediately involved in the letter.   His
only offence is in making the allegorical division cover
two types of meaning which, as Aquinas will presently
show, are widely different.

To appreciate the rigour and yet the broad sanity of
St. Thomas's own scheme of Scriptural interpretation,
it is necessary to recall once more the distinction to
which I have already referred between words as signifying things and the things thus signified as in turn
signifying other things.   Now, the literal sense of
Scripture is confined to the things signified by its

actual words, and it embraces all such things. Every shade of meaning, therefore, which can be shown to be legitimately implied in the words of Scripture is part of its literal sense. But where those things become themselves symbols of other things we enter at once upon the spiritual sense. It is, indeed, called spiritual just because it is a knowledge of invisible things mediated through the natural symbolism of the visible world. But this spiritual meaning, though one in kind by reason of its general symbolic character, is actually of different species in virtue of the different nature of the things symbolised. For the truth thus symbolically revealed to us was revealed in order to guide us either to right belief or to right action. All the symbolism that has the latter purpose yields the moral or tropological sense of Scripture. But where it is a question of symbols signifying things to be believed, it is necessary to make a distinction of value in the symbols themselves. The visible things signified by words become, as we have shown, symbols of invisible things. But those invisible things themselves can become the symbols of still higher spiritual realities.

Let us take, for instance, the hierarchy represented by the Synagogue, the Church on earth, and the Church Triumphant. Now here we have the Old Testament as figure of the New, so that all that is spoken there of the Law and the Synagogue is to be interpreted symbolically of Christ and the Church. Such knowledge belongs to the strictly allegorical meaning of Scripture. But all the facts of Christ's life on earth, whether foreshadowed in the Old Testament or ful-

filled in the New, all that is said of the Church whether
in prophecy or in fulfilment, become in turn symbols
through which is mediated to us the further knowledge
of the Church Triumphant.   This is the anagogical
meaning, the crown and climax of all revealed
knowledge.

Now it may reasonably be objected that such a
scheme of interpretation has no actual value for us,
that it is the purely fantastic construction of a habit of
mind which we have definitely left behind and is never
likely to be revived.   But even if its intrinsic interest
should be little more than archæological, I think it is
still important as witness to a religious attitude and
requirement which profoundly impressed the whole
character of Christian theology.   What the Middle
Age so earnestly and eagerly strained to find in Revelation was a sure guide to the fullest knowledge of the
Divine Nature which was at all possible for man here
on earth, and that just because in such knowledge
alone did man's real blessedness consist.   When the
mediæval theologian spoke of man's salvation he did
not mean merely his deliverance from the bondage of
sin.   That was but the negative limit beyond which
lay the life with God, the only true blessedness.   All
else in religion was but means which made this heavenly conversation possible, a figure which pointed on to
its reality.   True religion was such all-absorbing and
possessive desire of the Divine perfections as could be
fulfilled only in the life of contemplation, a life which
included the active life and gave it all its value.   To
dwell habitually with the good and the true in contemplation of the Supreme Good and the Supreme

Truth—such was the ideal of mediæval religion. Hence its conviction that Revelation was fulfilled in its anagogical meaning which admitted, even if still as through a mirror, to a knowledge of the Divine mysteries.

Yet it is just here that the fundamental sanity of mediæval theology shines out most clearly. It never forgets that we are here *in statu pupillari* and that Revelation is a condescension to our limited capacity for learning. The mystical theology which would penetrate to the ultimate secrets of Revelation must therefore be kept in due subjection to dogmatic theology which is the interpretation of the letter. And so we must put ourselves to school under the Divine Teacher in a spirit of uttermost simplicity and teachableness to learn the literal meaning of Scripture, what the Teacher had actually said, before we can hope to understand any of its spiritual meanings, what the Teacher wishes ultimately to convey. Now it is the sole function of dogmatic theology to exhibit the whole system of revealed truth as founded on the literal meaning only. There is no principle of interpretation on which Aquinas is more insistent than that no theological argument can legitimately proceed from any spiritual meaning. Every spiritual meaning is a conclusion, never a premiss. And if it be objected that all spiritual meanings must then remain uncertain and conjectural only, owing to the weakness of our human reasoning, his answer is ready. There is no spiritual meaning contained under any letter of Scripture which is not elsewhere given in the letter. God has not

F

allowed any spiritual meaning which it is necessary for us to apprehend to remain dependent upon our uncertain interpretations.

But, as we have seen in the case of the division attempted by St. Augustine, there may still lurk much confusion between what is really literal meaning and what is in the strict sense spiritual. This confusion Aquinas sets himself carefully to remove. In the first place not all that is figurative pertains necessarily to the allegorical meaning. The letter of human language is largely figurative and must of necessity be so. It is only in virtue of this figurative character of human language that we can adequately express any general truth or suggest any invisible reality. And Holy Scripture is especially rich in these metaphorical forms of expression, all of which belong organically to its literal meaning. In other words, the letter of Scripture does not mean the letter in its merely grammatical sense, letter as opposed to figure and stripped, so far as that is possible, of all relation to figure. It means the truth that comes to us directly through all the concrete richness of words, the thing which their subtlest use of metaphorical imagery is intended to express.

But the allegorical meaning is of an altogether different species from the metaphorical. The metaphor is no doubt the use of a thing to represent another thing. But the representing thing is chosen only because of its aptitude to make the thing represented more vividly present to the mind. Its value is exhausted in its figurative or representative capacity. But it is when a thing has revelational value in itself

and is also the symbol of a further revelational value
that the allegorical meaning for the first time emerges.
Thus, when God is described as a Rock or a Lion, the
obvious similitudes of the Divine trustworthiness or
the Divine might have no value beyond their more
vigorous suggestion of those qualities in God.   Indeed, as St. Thomas somewhat naïvely explains,
Scriptural metaphors seem to have been taken deliberately from the lowliest and most familiar objects
in order to obviate all possibility of conceiving their
relations to the Divine Nature with a too grammatical
literalness.   When Scripture speaks of the arm of the
Lord, no direct statement could describe God's
operative virtue with the force and cogency which
this image gives to it, and yet not even the simplest
and most unlettered reader of Holy Scripture could be
tempted to take it for anything more than an image.
Allegory, as I have said, is of an entirely different order
from this purely descriptive device of metaphor.   It
is a meaning within a meaning.   Thus Old Testament
narrative and prophecy have distinct revelational
value of their own, yet are also allegories of the revelation of the Gospel, just as both are in addition to
their own literal value as revelation symbolical also of
the secret mysteries of the heavenly Kingdom.

A similar distinction has to be made with regard to
the tropological or moral sense.   Scripture consists
in very large measure of directly moral teaching.
The Divine condescension to our need is nowhere
exhibited more manifestly than in the care with which
Scripture rehearses for us once again the most elementary dictates of the Law of Nature, thus investing

them with a Divine sacredness and authority which we might not otherwise have ascribed to them. Now all this moral teaching belongs quite obviously to the letter, and Aquinas is careful to impress upon us that it has nothing to do with what he means by the *sensus moralis*. That sense is confined to the higher region of duty which is symbolised for us in certain events of Holy Scripture, especially in the events of our Lord's earthly life, and which is enjoined upon us by that symbolism. St. Paul has made that spiritual meaning again literal, has translated it into the letter, when he speaks of our being buried with Christ in baptism, of our being crucified with Him and dying unto sin, of our rising again with Him and setting our hearts on the things that are above, of our dwelling with Him in the heavenly places. The drama of our Lord's earthly life, itself the fulfilment of the prophetic symbolism of the Old Testament, thus becomes the further symbolic presentation and as it were rehearsal of the fully Christian life in action. The moral sense of Scripture, therefore, in the strict sense to which Aquinas confines it, is definitely one of those spiritual senses which are hidden in some statement of the letter, though always literally revealed in some other statement.

We are now, I think, in a position to resume the mediæval conception of Revelation, a conception which survived with a practical integrity till almost our own day. The Divine Revelation is given in the Scriptures of the Old and New Testaments and in a penumbra of tradition authentically proceeding from contemporary memories of our Lord's life and teach-

ing. Nothing else has revelational value, *i.e.* possesses that Divine authority in virtue of which it may
be regarded as belonging to those infallible first principles on which theology is founded.   No later interpretation, however divinely assisted, has such value or
authority.   However fully deserving of respect the
great body of patristic interpretation may be, however
closely it may be and ought to be followed as a guide,
it must never be confused with Revelation itself.   Yet
interpretation and theology have a very distinctive
function to fulfil.   For God revealed Himself only
that we might have the Divinely assured and infallible
first principles of all possible knowledge of Him.
This knowledge we may further deduce by aid of the
reason working on these *principia*, never indeed with
the certitude of faith which is given to Revelation only,
but with a degree of probability which is always the
higher the more constantly theology returns for con-
firmation to the revealed data.

Now, Scripture consists of teaching and of narrative.
The teaching is Divine teaching.   The narrative is the
narrative of the Divine action in history.   Both have
the same purpose, the Divine education of the human
race.   But the Divine action has the fuller and deeper
significance in that it is symbolical, and symbolical in
a manifold fashion.   The Old Law is throughout the
figure of the New.   That is its unique revelational
value and its unique character as history.   The *Gesta
Dei per Hebraeos*, the lives of the Patriarchs from Adam
and Seth to Abraham, Isaac and Jacob, the long and
varied history of the People of the Covenant, the work
of lawgiver and chronicler and prophet—all these are

immediate revelations of the Divine mind and purpose. But they are also pregnant with a fuller meaning which in the fulness of time is declared literally in the Gospel. Once again, the literal revelation of both the Old Law and the New, their revelation in events, contains within it the hidden mysteries of the heavenly Kingdom, of God and His eternal order. Wheresoever, to use the words of St. Gregory, Holy Scripture narrates an event, it is also setting forth a mystery. *Ubi narrat gestum, prodit mysterium.* It is the function of interpretation to seek out these hidden meanings of theology, to classify and systematise them. And both, to discharge their functions aright, must carefully observe the rule that every one of their conclusions is to be tried by its accordance with some literal declaration of Scripture.

Finally, to the symbolical value of events in Holy Scripture must be added their evidential value. They are not only vehicles of the fullest Divine teaching, but also all-convincing evidence that the teaching is of God. The Old Testament history contains within itself every meaning which it was the Divine intention to reveal. But in that it is miraculous and prophetic throughout, it is also its own sufficient witness as a Divine Revelation. Its events have a prophetic character which is both external and internal. They announce the Divine future and they symbolise it. The Synagogue heralds the Gospel, but it also already contains it in figure. Christ not only comes as the fulness of time, as the fulfilment of every Divine event which the Old Testament narrates ; He has also Himself appeared in each of those events, in the long series of theophanies which lie between Adam and His own earthly advent as Messiah; and His own earthly manifestation is in turn both prophecy and symbol of the completed Divine purpose as it exists for ever in the Eternal Order. This is history as the Middle Age conceived it and was alone interested in it, the unfoldment in time of the *totum atque simul* of God's eternal moment. Holy Scripture approves its character as authentically Divine Revelation by the fact that it is history on this Divine scale. Prophecy and miracle are not mere accidental accompaniments authenticating one portion of its contents by another. They are the stuff of which it is woven throughout. The greatest of all miracles, says St. Thomas, is the miracle which made Revelation possible, the miracle by which God so enlightened the human mind as to make it capable of receiving His truth. In its conception of Revelation the mediæval world did not certainly fail to do justice to the self-evidencing character of Holy Scripture as revealed truth. The next chapter will be concerned principally with the modifications and extensions of that conception effected by the Reformers.

SYNOPSIS OF CHAPTER V

Exclusively Scriptural foundation of the Christian religion as firmly asserted by Middle Age as by Reformation. Principal change wrought by Reformation in the matter of Scripture the extension of knowledge of it beyond the ranks of the *clerici* by translation into the vulgar tongues. Popular teaching of Scripture brings about, too, a certain change of stress, as, *e.g.*, in use of the word *salvation*. The Reformers did not indeed exclude from its meaning the *end*, the *fruitio Dei*, but none the less concentrated, it might seem disproportionately, on the *means*. Luther specially representative of this stress and of the discrimination within Scripture which corresponded with it.

Calvin, exact and careful theologian, keeps close to the mediæval tradition while developing it with peculiar force in a new and vigorous French prose. Admirable recapitulation of the revealing guidance in the transmission of the Divine Word throughout the ages, the miraculous attestations in its deliverance, preservation, universal authority, and consentient witness of the Church.

Point of Calvin's departure from tradition, his denial of sufficiency to these and all other merely external motives of credibility. Scripture must, to be fully Revelation and not the mere archives of a past Revelation, have in itself a living witness to its own character. This witness it has in the Divine Spirit whose ever-present voice it is.

This departure from mediæval doctrine most clearly marked in different conception of the rôle of faith in Revelation. Faith for Aquinas, though itself a Divine gift, merely enabled from without acceptance of the different Divine gift of Revelation. In Calvin's conception they are not separable. God's Revelation produces faith and is vitally received by man *as* faith, not after an antecedent act of faith in its Divine character.

In addition to religious motive for Calvin's insistence on internal witness there may have been also an apologetic motive in the menace to historical credibility already apparent in critical temper of Renaissance. He himself at least clearly recognises that menace and undertakes detailed refutation of the objections urged, but admits powerlessness of all such arguments against him who does not will to believe. Progress of criticism after Calvin.

V. THE REFORMATION AND SCRIPTURE

THE popular view that the Reformation was the recovery of the Scriptural character of the Christian Religion is one of those half-truths which our great Victorian poet justly characterised as " ever the blackest of lies." The measure of truth which it contains is that the Reformation coincided with and was also the direct occasion of an immense widening and enlargement of the popular knowledge of Holy Scripture. The Reformation was, largely in intention, still more largely in effect, the transplantation of the monastic ideal into the world of ordinary secular life. If within the sphere of its influence it suppressed the monastic orders, it was mainly because it held the double standard of the religious life which monasticism perpetuated to be a source of religious weakness and unreality. The service of God was in its fulness possible for all and therefore binding upon all. If the monastic ideal required the acceptance of vows which were clearly incompatible with the conditions of life in the world, those vows were thereby convicted of being unnecessary to the fully Christian life. But in all other respects the life of the Christian in the world needed to be attuned to the ascetic perfection at which monasticism had aimed.

To this end the Reformers conceived it as their first duty to make the knowledge of Holy Scripture possible

for all. That knowledge had necessarily been confined hitherto to the *clerici*, to those who had been
trained in the monastic schools in the familiar use of
the Latin language. How widely it was in fact extended among that class every student of mediæval
literature is well aware. The text of the Vulgate was
almost as familiar to the general body of half-lettered
clerks in the Middle Age as the text of the English
Bible is to us, or at least was to our immediate forefathers. But it is unnecessary to underline the immense extension of that knowledge which was effected
by the translation of the Biblical text into the vulgar
tongues. It was, indeed, these translations more than
any other cause, perhaps more than all other causes
put together, which helped to transform two at least
of these tongues of the people, the English and the
German, into the instruments of great classical
literatures.

In so far, therefore, as the claim made on behalf
of the Reformation is meant to suggest or imply
that the exclusively Scriptural foundation of the
Christian religion had been previously undervalued
or depressed, it is almost grotesquely unjust. But,
on the other hand, it is abundantly true that the
widest popular knowledge and use of the revealed
Word date from and were a direct result of the
period of religious controversy which the Reformation
inaugurated. And it is also true that this popular
use did of itself tend to modify certain features of the
traditional scheme of interpretation which was described in the last chapter. Such modifications were
none the less important because largely unconscious

rather than deliberate and intentional. And it may be possible to trace something of their character and importance in the retrospect where both remained comparatively obscure for their immediate agents. That at any rate is what I now propose to attempt.

The change of which one is most conscious in passing from mediæval to reformed theology is a change of accent. For both alike man's blessedness is *in* God, whether it be described with Augustine as the fruition or with Aquinas as the vision of God, whether it be conceived of as predominantly volitional or as predominantly intellectual. And here it is to be observed that the language of the reformers is always by preference Augustinian, partly because of the special devotion of the Reformers to the theologian of grace, but partly also no doubt owing to the influence, especially upon Luther, of the voluntarism of the later mediæval philosophy with which the language of Augustine was more readily accordant. Again for both mediæval and reformed theology there was only one means by which man could attain to blessedness, the revealed economy of the Incarnation as God's work of redemption. But mediæval theology did deliberately stress the end where just as deliberately the reformed stressed the means. Thus the very word *salvation*, the key-word of religion, underwent a modification of meaning, however slight. For St. Thomas it was definitely the consummation in blessedness of the whole process of redemptive grace. Or if it were by him equated with the work of redemption it was definitely as the earthly arc of a circle which could only be completed in the heavenly order. It

would be unfair to say of the Reformers, and especially
of Calvin who was a not unworthy successor of the
great mediæval theologians, that they altogether
omitted from their purview this completion of the
heavenly circle as man's true end. This, as Christian
theologians, it was impossible for them to do. Yet
not only as popular religious teachers, but also as
professed theologians, they did concentrate upon the
way of salvation, the means of redemption as the *unum
necessarium* of religion.

Now it will be at once evident how this change of
stress affected the Reformers' attitude towards and use
of the traditional methods of interpretation. Almost
as a matter of course the anagogical and moral
meanings lost all their importance. The allegorical
meaning, indeed, remained in all its force. The type-
character of the Old Testament as the prophecy of
Redemption in symbolic events was even developed
with a new thoroughness. But even the Old Testament was valuable less as allegorical meaning than as
prophetic and evidential witness to the truth that was
to be fully and directly declared in the Gospel. The
Reformers made full use of the mediæval principle of
interpretation that no spiritual meaning was to be
accepted as having the authority of revelation which
had not its literal analogue in some other portion of
Scripture. It was these literal meanings which they
sought out and invested with a unique authority.

Luther especially discriminated this Bible within the
Bible. In St. Paul he discovered every anagogical,
moral, or even allegorical meaning which might lie
concealed in the dark places of Scripture, revealed in

all the satisfying clearness of the letter.   St. Paul alone
had unambiguously declared the redeeming Christ,
and in that declaration all Scripture had been fulfilled.
But in thus discriminating between Scripture and
Scripture, Luther was not merely following the
mediæval scheme of interpretation.   It is even possible that that scheme was not consciously present to
his mind.   He was rather introducing almost a new
conception of Revelation itself.   His own experience
had taught him that God spoke directly in His Word
to the heart of the believer.   That, of course, was the
experience also of an Augustine, a Francis of Assisi,
and many another Christian soul both before and
after him.   But Luther was not content to take it as
a perfectly natural subjective experience of the
individual believer.   With the impulsive self-con-
fidence which characterised him, he proceeded to
erect it into an objective criterion of Revelation.   The
Pauline Gospel which had revealed to him what
Christ was, was the Word of God in the fullest sense.
All else in Scripture was but preparatory and subsidiary revelation.   Strange as it may sound, no
Christian doctor of the front rank ever disparaged the
revelational rôle of Scripture more consistently than
the great Reformer.   It was he who had the daring
to say, " It is for Christ's sake that we believe in the
Scriptures, not for the Scriptures' sake that we believe in Christ."

Calvin was a great theologian with a reasoned
respect for theological tradition where Luther was a
religious genius brusquely impatient of it.   Yet it was
Calvin's carefully elaborated theory, not Luther's

occasional outbursts, that determined the Reformed attitude towards Scripture. For Calvin, as for the great mediæval theologians, the Bible was throughout the self-revealing Word of God. From the first moment of creation God had revealed Himself in the fulness of His nature to Adam. He had renewed that revelation after the Fall in all the patriarchs from Seth till Noah, and again in the covenant with Abraham and his seed, in the Law and the Prophets, until every partial theophany was fulfilled in the Advent of the very Word itself made flesh. The authority of Scripture was the self-evidence of its Divine origin and character. The knowledge it gave was a knowledge to which man of himself could never have attained. That knowledge was so uniformly consistent and so intimately correlated in its different parts that only the wantonly perverse could doubt that it proceeded from a single mind. It revealed in its different portions and divers manners the one truth of the Divine Nature in its relations with man of which every idolatrous image of that Nature which man himself had formed was a blasphemous travesty. And not only the content of the Revelation but every circumstance of its communication was an inexpugnable proof of its Divine character. Its human instruments, as, for instance, Moses, were designated as such by the miraculous powers conferred upon them as signs of their Divine mission. The prophets were the human vehicles of a knowledge which only God could give, not only of events still hidden in the womb of time but of the eternal secrets of God reflected in the mirror of their inspired vision.

And when we come to the New Testament, who will dare to deny that the three Evangelists (it is interesting to note already the distinction of the Synoptics from the Fourth Gospel), though they tell their story in a plain, unvarnished style, *en style bas*, yet transcend all human capacity in setting forth the heavenly mysteries ? The most hardened of sceptics must be confounded if he will only read the first chapter of St. Luke.   But it is for St. John that Calvin reserves the mightiest rôle as an instrument of revelation.   " Thundering as it were from heaven," he says, " he must reduce every soul to the obedience of faith."   The critics who revel in eradicating from the human heart all reverence for Scripture will, when they have read St. John, find his words burning into their consciences with the flame that will speedily consume their ribald mockery.   As for St. Peter and St. Paul, their doctrine is possessed of such a heavenly majesty that not even the most rebellious souls can long resist its constraining power.

Then, too, there is the miraculous preservation of Scripture throughout so many ages from all the devices which the forces of evil had prepared from time to time for its destruction, the recovery of the Law in the time of Josiah, the failure of the edict of Antiochus who, as we are told in the First Book of the Maccabees, ordered all copies of it to be destroyed, its literal integrity throughout all the changes and chances of time.   Even more wonderful, perhaps, was the fact that in the Divine providence the preservation of Scripture was entrusted to a people that did not know the fulness of its meaning, that, as St. Augustine says, the greatest enemies of the Gospel should have been librarians of the records which were its credentials. Finally, the Divine origin of Scripture was attested by the immediate authority which it exercised over so many different peoples varying most widely in custom and tradition, and by its power of drawing them all to embrace with joy the exacting discipline of that Divine manner of life which it proposed to them.

Now, all these were no doubt only the common-places of mediæval theology, but stated with the fresh-ness and vigour of one whom all historians of French literature have piously recognised as the first great master of French prose. But Calvin himself refused to concede to them any fully convincing character. He was quite aware that they could never bring con-viction to the unbelieving or even the naturally in-credulous. To those who believed already on other grounds they were indeed supporting buttresses of the reasoned structure of their belief. But the fully sufficient motives and grounds of belief in the revealed word must be of a Divine, not human, character and origin. They must be themselves revealed. That of course, too, the mediæval theologians had abun-dantly held and taught in their doctrine that faith is the free gift of God. Calvin is again only repeating them when he says that no one can believe the Scriptures to be of God except by faith. " Cela ne se cognoist que par foy." But he gives an amplitude to this doctrine which had not been necessary or even per-haps possible in the thirteenth century. Faith was, as we have seen, for St. Thomas a merely initial adhesion to the Divine Word and its promises which

word and therefore infallible truth. It was, in the figure which St. Thomas customarily used to represent it, the schoolboy's acceptance on the authority of his master of truths which he cannot himself yet fully comprehend. True, he receives them thus in order that he may proceed, with a still fuller measure of the Divine assistance, to make them his own, in order that his *fides informis* may become a *fides formata*. But it remains that faith is given by God to enable an independent act of adhesion to the Revelation which He has already given. In other words, Revelation and Faith are both gifts of grace, but they are different gifts. In order that God's gift of Revelation might be recognised as such, there was needed another distinctive Divine act in the recognising soul. And that act might include and even require the presentation of certain human motives of credibility.

Now Calvin, as I have said, marshalled these motives of belief with a singular fulness and force. But he felt in an even greater degree than Aquinas and the whole mediæval world had felt that rational motives were not sufficient to the acceptance of something so unique as an infallible Divine Revelation. Only God Himself could provide the fully sufficient motive. The fully sufficient witness to Scripture as Divine Revelation must be something more than a faith that the Revelation long since given was really of God, even though that faith was also a gift of God. It must be a witness inherent in Scripture here and now, making it God's Revelation here and now. Witness and that which was witnessed to must be one everpresent Divine act. That was what Calvin meant by the witness of the Spirit. The Holy Scriptures are not just the carefully preserved Divine archives which may be consulted for a knowledge of what God once spoke, to, or even through, the Prophets. They are the living Word, the actual voice of God speaking in every now in the secret ear of men's hearts. The Spirit who spake by the Prophets is still speaking through them, and only Scripture as this immediate utterance of the Spirit is fully and authentically Revelation. The witness of the Spirit *to* Revelation is simply the fact that the Spirit speaks *in* Revelation. If through the words of Holy Scripture the *Vox Dei* does not penetrate, then those words have ceased to be the Word. Thus the Spirit is no merely external witness to the Divine origin and authority of a word which God had spoken in some distant past. It is the witness to Scripture because it is the living voice that makes Scripture a present Revelation.

But Calvin insists further that the words spoken by the Spirit are not only a Revelation, but the only Revelation. Not unnaturally the importance attached by the Reformers to the witness of the Spirit provoked excesses which might undermine the very foundations of the Christian tradition. Why should God be bound to His own past utterances? Why should He not reveal Himself now as indubitably as in the days of the Fathers, and independently of the revelation made to them? Or again, now that the preparatory message of the prophets had been fulfilled in the Gospel, why should we any longer attribute to them a revelational value which clearly ought to be reserved exclusively for the Revelation which they

heralded and was now declared in Christ ?   It will be
seen that Luther's own example might be pleaded as
justifying at any rate this latter position.   But Calvin's
conception of Revelation, *i.e.* his conception of God
and of His relations with men, was much too mediæval
to allow for a moment of such radical imperilling of
the Christian tradition.   In creating man God had
given him the revelation of His true nature which he
would need to the end of time.   His revelation, like
His knowledge, was a *totum simul*.   As given to the
Patriarchs, as renewed in the covenant with Abraham
and his seed, as declared in the Law and the Prophets,
as fulfilled in Christ, it was one single revelation of
the Divine knowledge necessary for man's salvation.
Then, no doubt, the Spirit dispensed it in varying
measure to the minds of men just as He did now.
Some understood then, as some understand now,
more fully than others.   Some were more responsive
than others to the teaching of the Spirit.   But it was
the same Spirit who taught, and it was the same
Revelation, the Revelation fulfilled in Christ, which
He taught.

The Spirit might, indeed, have revealed Himself
directly to certain elect souls on special occasions, for
guidance in some special need or to call them to some
notable service or even to illuminate their under-
standings with a new apprehension of Divine truth.
But no such private and particular revelation, the
Middle Age consistently held, had the revelational
value of Holy Scripture.   Theology could not accept
it as among the first principles of its reasoning.   And
further, whatever revelational value it might really

possess must be already contained explicitly in Scripture. The old doctrine of the supremacy of control vested in the literal meaning had fresh application here. Calvin therefore was true to the tradition of mediæval theology when he identified Scripture as the exclusive field of the Spirit's illumination. That was not to confine the Spirit's action. It was, on the contrary, to recognise it as His action. For Revelation was *ex hypothesi* God's whole purpose for man declared to man. And the Spirit Who had declared the whole must remain within it to declare afresh its meaning for every instance of human need whether individual or social. The Spirit's guidance of the Church as of the individual Christian was a guidance from within the all-exclusive and all-sufficient Word which He, the Divine Wisdom, had spoken unto man from the beginning and would speak unto the end.

Now it was this virtual identification of God's Spirit and God's Word as the sum of His relations with man that constituted the distinguishing originality of Calvin's teaching and through him has affected profoundly the religious outlook of the Protestant world ever since. It is among the ironies of history that its effect has declared itself in a literalism of interpretation before unknown, a literalism, indeed, which it was its chief purpose to guard against as a betrayal of the genuinely religious integrity of Scripture. But if Calvin's doctrine was directed against a mere literalist fundamentalism, it was, on the other hand, the chief bulwark of what I may call a historic fundamentalism, an unquestioning belief in the exact historical truth of Scripture as guaranteed by its Divine authorship.

This character, indeed, it has shared with the consistent doctrine of the Roman schools, vigorously restated and reinforced in the Vatican decree of 1870. But whereas in the Roman Church it has been effectually screened by the authority of the Church in defining dogma, in Protestantism it has stood out in bold and, until recently, defiant relief. Yet it is noteworthy that Calvin's treatment of the whole question in the first book of the *Institution* bears witness already to the imminence of the critical attack which was to undermine historic fundamentalism. It would be possible, indeed, to reconstruct from those few chapters of his not only the main outlines but also most of the details of Renaissance criticism of the traditional doctrine, the reasoned doubts it alleged against the reputed authorship of many of the books of the Old Testament or their received dates, or, again, against the historical value of its narrative. And though he often dismisses these doubts with the contemptuous impatience of the convinced believer, yet he betrays his sense of their danger not only by the carefully reasoned arguments with which he supports his righteous scorn but also and especially by his determined refusal to admit any kind of sufficiency in historic motives of credibility. His witness of the Spirit is quite obviously not only a confession of his profoundly religious evaluation of Scripture, but is also for him the only trustworthy barrier against a merely historical and therefore critical examination of its contents.

With the beginning of the next century, however, historical inquiry was being taken more seriously even by earnest believers and was forcing them back once again, as in the case of Grotius, upon the need of authority in interpretation. By the middle of the seventeenth century an honest critical reading of patristic texts had persuaded scholars like the Jesuit Petavius and the Oratorian Thomassin that there had been wide variation in early patristic interpretation, variation so wide and deep that writers like Tertullian and Athenagoras, who had been always esteemed orthodox, would have been convicted of heresy if they had written after the conciliar period instead of before it. And so the way was prepared for the Father of Biblical criticism, the great Oratorian Richard Simon, in whose history of interpretation even more than in his critical histories of the Old and New Testaments were contained already the main outlines of that historical treatment of Scripture which has extended now over two centuries.

Let us in conclusion consider how theology has met the critical attack. To that end it will be necessary to confront the dogmatic requirements of the one with the reasoned conclusions of the other. Theology requires the belief that in the Scriptures of the Old and New Testaments God has directly revealed to man all the truths necessary for his salvation. Throughout its classical period it further consistently assumed that God had given that Revelation as His own account of His relations with man in giving effect to that saving purpose from the beginning to the end of time. This is what I have called the historic fundamentalism of the classical theology, whether Catholic or Protestant. And, finally, it

assumed that the Divine origin and authority of this
Revelation were sufficiently attested by the texture of
miracle and prophecy of which it was in large measure
composed. On the other hand, criticism demonstrated the existence in Holy Scripture and throughout
all its parts of a contingent and human element which
seemed quite inconsistent with its integrity as Divine
Revelation. Now theology has met the assaults of
criticism in three different ways. When Bossuet
launched his determined attack against what he regarded as Richard Simon's blasphemous denial of
the infallibility and inerrancy of Holy Scripture, the
Oratorian Scholar replied that the critical conclusions
to which he had been forced by a linguistic and historical study of the Biblical documents might, indeed,
be fatal to Protestantism as resting on the authority
of Scripture alone, but were harmless for the Roman
Church, which claimed to be the infallible interpreter
of Scripture. To Bossuet it seemed a cynically
sceptical plea which only added to Simon's offence in
his eyes. Yet Simon had the true prevision of the
line which Catholic apologetic was to take. Rome
could not, of course, admit the legitimacy of Simon's
conclusions or of the further developments to which
they were to lead. It officially repudiated the whole
critical position as heresy at the Vatican Council. But
it was able to do so because of its belief in the rôle of
the Catholic and Apostolic Church, which it claimed
to represent exclusively, as the infallible interpreter of
Scripture.

The second way in which theology has attempted
to overcome the critical attack is that of Karl Barth

and his disciples.   Just as the Vatican method was a
logical development of the mediæval motives of
credibility, so is the Barthian a development of
Calvin's witness of the Spirit.   Its advantage is that
it can and does admit the generally accepted results of
criticism while proclaiming the fully revelational
character of Holy Scripture.   Whatever the historical
contingencies through which God has spoken, it is
His authentic voice for which we listen and which we
actually hear in Scripture.   For religion Scripture is
the word which He has spoken once and for all, yet
is always speaking afresh, to the utmost range of
human need.   Barthianism, therefore, rather than the
idolatrous worship of the letter of popular Protestantism would seem to be the true development of the
Reformed conception of Scripture.

Finally, there was the frank return to the self-
evidencing character of Revelation in its structure of
miracle and prophecy, most ably represented in the
vigorous reasoning of J. B. Mozley's Bampton
Lectures of 1865.   This was neither the evasion nor
the acceptance of criticism, but the belated denial of
either legitimacy in its methods or value in its conclusions.   In the next chapter I hope to deal more
fully with the value of these attempts before con-
sidering generally the present position of the Christian
belief in Revelation.

SYNOPSIS OF CHAPTER VI

Christian Revelation never treated as merely oracular for two reasons. First, Christian theology always held more or less closely to the view of the created order itself as distantly revelatory of the Divine perfections. Secondly, the Revelation of Holy Scripture had been given largely through events in time. Thus Scripture assumed the character of a Divine history, the history of humanity as seen from God's side and indeed as narrated by Him.

The offence of Biblical Criticism, that it seemed to challenge this view so long and deeply rooted in the Christian consciousness. Theology, forced to meet this challenge, has in fact met it either (1) by refusing the right of criticism to enter the sacred domain of Scripture, or (2) by so revising the conception of Revelation that the results of criticism need no longer be in conflict with it.

Two examples of (1) selected and considered : J. B. Mozley's bold restatement of the traditional conception in its most rigorous form in the opening lecture of his Bamptons of 1865 ; and the Vatican Decrees of 1870. Both simple reaffirmations of tradition without explicit reference to criticism.

Barthian theology taken as example of (2). Here the results of criticism, regarded as constituting a problem, seem to be simply ignored. Accepted rather as one of the facts in the general situation to be considered. Tendency, indeed, to regard them as helpful to true view of Revelation. That view would seem to be an affirmation of Calvin's " witness of the Spirit " in its utmost rigour, without even Calvin's measure of regard for external motives of credibility. Religiously impressive, but philosophically weak in its assertion of Divine authority in Revelation as the supersession, or even suppression, of every active human quality in receiving it. Scripture itself, and notably the fact and doctrine of the Incarnation, witness against such a view of the nature of Divine authority in Revelation. Religious belief cannot be founded on mere nihilism in spheres of psychology and history. Cutting theological knots an evidence of human weakness and impatience. They must be patiently unravelled.

VI. TRADITION AND CRITICISM

THE primary claim of Christianity is that it is the self-revelation of God to man in a Person who is His Word. It is in virtue of this claim that the Christian Revelation has a quite unique character of its own. For the Word of God was conceived of as having uttered itself not only in all the theophanies of the Old Testament, not only in Jesus Christ as their fulfilment, but also and first of all in the whole created order. This conception of Creation as the Divine utterance extended Revelation into the domain of contingent events which made up the whole history of the Cosmos. No mere series of oracles, such as were given, for instance, in the Koran or in the prophetic portions of the Old Testament, could contain the wholeness of the revelation which God had actually given. Even the conception of a special revelation of truths beyond the attainment of man's unaided reason did not annul this wider character of revelation. It merely supplemented a revelation already given to reason. We have seen how fully this truth was recognised by the mediæval Augustinian tradition in its rational quest of the Divine *vestigia* in creation. And in Scotus Erigena the principle had been carried to still further and more radical applications. That very original thinker was daring enough to plant reason at the heart of all revelation and to constitute it as the final interpretative authority thereof. I know of no Christian writing better worth pondering to-day in this connection than the introductory chapters of the *De Divisione Naturae*. I am not sure, indeed, that we may not have to go back to something like the position of Erigena for a conception of revelation which will satisfy the demands of reason without sacrificing indispensable requirements of religion.

Another feature of the Scriptural Revelation which gave it a more than oracular character was its mediation through what purported to be a universal history of mankind. This, however, unlike its character of a supra-rational extension of the revelation already given to reason, is exactly its chief difficulty for us of to-day. But so long as it was possible to conceive of history in the Eastern and mediæval fashion as having no importance other than that of a medium for the declaration in events of the Divine purpose, it was the supreme distinction of Scripture as revelation that it had this character. Just as God had revealed Himself in nature to the inquiring reason, so had He revealed Himself more intimately still in history. If nature was the utterance of the Word in things, history was its utterance in acts. How immensely satisfying this view of revealed history, of history seen only from its Godward side, could be, even as late as the end of the seventeenth century, we have abundant proof in that last great masterpiece of history so conceived and written— Bossuet's *Discours sur l'histoire universelle*. But with the eighteenth century history in the modern sense, after a period of gestation which had lasted since the

Renaissance, was born into the clear light of day. At the very moment that Bossuet was composing the last great anthem of history as the earthly texture of the Divine harmonies, Richard Simon was lisping the first numbers of its all-too-human and this-worldly reality, and just, too, where that reality was most disturbingly intrusive.

Now, it is all-important to recognise the real character of this disturbance. Calvin's witness of the Spirit had degenerated throughout the Protestant world into what I have called a literal fundamentalism, by which I mean just what is otherwise described as the theory of verbal inspiration. But behind this literal fundamentalism there lay the conception of Scripture as Divine history, as the integral history of humanity seen from God's side. Now the offence of criticism was that it seemed to destroy this character of Scripture altogether, that it did in fact so reduce it as to make confident belief in the conception impossible. Whatever the hopes and labours of theologians in blunting the force of the critical attack might be, on the popular side it had one of two effects—either the total loss of belief in Revelation or the repudiation of criticism as an inadmissible and indeed blasphemous interference in the Divine realm. It ought not to be surprising to us that this has been the case. Just in proportion as religion was bound up with the belief in Revelation as Divine history, as it has been until quite recently throughout Christendom, whether Catholic or Protestant, it was indeed inevitable.

But it is, of course, with the efforts of theology to meet the critical assault that we are here concerned.

Let us first consider Dr. J. B. Mozley's argument in his famous lectures on Miracles. Mozley's brilliant defence of the credibility of miracle was indeed directed immediately against the scientific scepticism prevalent in his time. But that he had Biblical criticism also in mind, if only in the form of *Essays and Reviews* published five years earlier, is sufficiently apparent from his statement in the preface to the first edition of his book that one of the things he is opposing as " a peculiarity of the present time " is " a disposition to maintain the disbelief of miracles upon a religious basis and in connection with a declared belief in the Christian revelation." With Mozley's general argument we need concern ourselves only in its bearings upon the nature of Revelation and its credibility as Revelation. Now Mozley's contention is that these two questions cannot be disjoined. If Revelation is a Divine disclosure and communication of truths undiscoverable by the human reason, as he, with the consentient witness of Christian tradition, held it to be, then its Divine origin and character must be self-authenticating. And that authentication must consist in something in its own structure intended as evidence of such Divine origin and capable of being such evidence because something beyond the power of man. In other words, the supra-rational Revelation must be accompanied and attested by supra-human works, viz. miracles, including the miraculous gift of prophecy.

And Mozley pushes this necessity of miraculous attestation to its farthest limits by pushing also to its limits the supra-rational character of Revelation.

Those intrinsic characteristics and outward effects of Revelation on which we are most inclined to rely as motives and supports for our belief in it, its adaptation to the deepest needs of the human heart and its production of a unique quality of life, he decisively rejects as inadequate to such a purpose. " The human heart," he says, " responds to the doctrine of the Incarnation, and feels that doctrine to be adapted to it. But because the idea is thus adapted to it, is that a proof that it has been chosen in the Divine counsels to be put into execution ? No ; it would be wild reasoning to infer from the sublimity of a supposition, as a mere conception of the mind, that that conception had been embodied in a Divine dispensation, and to conclude from a thought of man an act of God. . . . So again, that the human heart responds to an Atonement supposed to be revealed is no proof that that Divine act has taken place ; because the human heart has no power by its mere longings of penetrating into the supernatural world and seeing what takes place there."

Mozley is willing to concede more evidential force to the moral results of the Christian Revelation. But their evidential weakness lies in the fact that they can never bear the whole burden of proof of the Divine character of the truth from which they issue. " If the sincere belief of persons in something does not prove that thing, can the natural consequences of that belief of themselves prove it ? If I am asked for the proof of a doctrine, and I say simply, ' I believe it,' that is obviously no proof ; but if I go on to say, 'This belief has had in my own case a connection with

H

devout practice,' that alone is not adequate proof
either, even though this connection has taken place in
others as well on a large scale." He then proceeds,
with the usual relentless honesty of his logic, to remind
his hearers that Christianity has had its moral failures
as well as its moral successes, that it has not succeeded
in stopping " war, persecution, tyranny, injustice, and
the dominion of selfish passion in the world which it
has professedly converted." That, no doubt, is not
the fault of Christianity, but of those who have called
themselves Christians. But, then, neither does it
justify resort to the fruits of Christianity as proof of
the Divine character of the Revelation on which it is
founded.

Mozley's argument, therefore, is the plea, urged
home with an extraordinary logical force, that reason
demands nothing less than a Divine, i.e. miraculous,
attestation of a Divine, i.e. supra-rational in the sense
of unattainable by human reason, Revelation. That
he may make his meaning unmistakable, he concludes
his first lecture by a contrast of Christianity with
Islam in which he convicts the founder of the latter
of an almost fatuous imbecility in offering to the
world a Revelation purporting to be Divine without
the accompaniment of miracle. I cannot refrain
from quoting him again, if only as evidence of the
depth of the abyss which yawns between us and a
really great theologian of not quite two generations
ago. " In this distinction alone between Mahometanism and Christianity we see a different estimate of
the claims of reason, lying at the foundation of these
religions and entertained by their respective founders.

Doubtless the founder of Mahometanism could have contrived false miracles had he chosen, but the fact that he did not consider miraculous evidence at all wanted to attest supernatural dispensation, but that his word was enough, shows an utterly barbarous idea of evidence and a total miscalculation of the claims of reason which unfits his religion for the acceptance of an enlightened age and people ; whereas the Gospel is adapted to perpetuity for this cause especially, with others, that it was founded upon a true calculation and a foresight of the permanent need of evidence ; our Lord admitting the inadequacy of His own mere word and the necessity of a rational guarantee to His revelation of His own nature and commission. ' If I had not done among them the works that none other man did, they had not had sin.' ' The works that I do bear witness of Me that the Father hath sent Me.' "

Now, the importance of Dr. Mozley's argument is that it presents with very great force and cogency the uniform Christian tradition as to the necessary credentials of Revelation. I have been careful to stress the other side of that tradition; its insistence that the Scriptural miracles and prophecy were evidential only, that it needed something more to receive the Revelation *as* Revelation, viz. the Divine gift of faith in it or the witness of the Spirit speaking through it. But both St. Thomas and Calvin were agreed that reasonable evidence of the revelational character of Scripture was necessary and that such evidence was forthcoming only in the miracles and prophecy through which it was given. Anything that called in question

the reality and force of these credentials would seem
to make faith or the witness of the Spirit entirely independent of reason.   That was Mozley's argument
which resumed the apologetic tradition of Christianity
up till his time.   Just because the truths communicated in Revelation were supra-rational, it was reasonable to expect and require sufficient evidence that
they had been Divinely given.   That evidence once
seriously called in question, faith in Revelation was
no longer reasonable.

The Fathers of the Vatican Council detected the
same danger in criticism, though they sought to avert
it in a slightly different fashion.   They held that the
initial act of faith in Scripture as Revelation would be
made more reasonable if it were transferred to the
infallible *magisterium* of the Church as the guardian of
Scripture.   But the validity of this attempt obviously
depended on the existence of equally cogent proofs of
the infallibility of that *magisterium*, proofs which were
not obviously forthcoming for those who considered
in a dispassionately critical spirit the circumstances of
its actual exercise in the course of history.   It was,
indeed, only too evident that the belief in this infallibility was an act of faith of exactly the same kind as the
faith in Scriptural Revelation of which it was proposed as the reasonable guarantee.   Further, belief
in the Church as the infallible guardian and interpreter of Scripture is for those who hold it an integral
part of the belief in Revelation itself.   It is only as
the fulfilment of a Divine Revelation that they assign
to the Church this Divine character and rôle.   If the
Church were a bare creature of history no one could,

and in so far as it is a creature of history no one can, claim for it this character. It is only because the Church is something more than a mere product of history, viz. the completion of a revealed Divine economy, that it can be in any sense the guarantee that the earlier steps of that economy are also Divine. The infallible Scriptures and the infallible Church are of one piece, woven throughout into one seamless garment. Neither can guarantee the Divine character of the other, save within the ambit of a faith which embraces them both. If reason is to be called in as a preliminary aid to faith, it must in the measure in which it can be such an aid at all guarantee them both on the same terms.

So far, then, the critical attack has been met by attempts to maintain the supra-rational, infallible, and inerrant character of Holy Scripture which tradition has held to be necessary to belief in it as Divine Revelation. But it is exactly that character which the results of a critical examination of its structure have called in question. Is it possible to accept the general validity of these results and yet continue to believe in it as authentically Divine Revelation ? To this question the answer of the Barthian theology is a confident affirmative. Now, I must confess that this theology, especially as expounded to us quite recently in England and to you, I believe, on this side of the Atlantic somewhat earlier by Dr. Brunner, makes a strong appeal to me. It does so in the first instance because it makes no attempt to minimise the measure of the human element which criticism has shown to exist in Holy Scripture, and secondly because in spite of this it needs, or thinks it needs, to make no slightest abatement in the traditional claim of a fully revelational quality and value for the Canonical Scriptures. And it has the additional merit of doing this by actually enhancing the religious quality of the faith which accepts the Word of God in Scripture. The faith which it postulates is still more obviously a Divine gift than the as yet unintelligent acceptance of revealed truth which alone tradition required in a *fides informis*. It is the faith of full discipleship, the faith which only the Divine Word resounding in the hushed silence of the expectant heart can awake. Faith, in short, is the attitude which the Word of God immediately evokes in every soul for whom it becomes His word. In the same act God speaks and the soul hears. The soul does not truly hear if it is not so overpowered and empowered by the majesty of the Word that it must forthwith turn away from self and towards God.

And again I find this theology attractive in its sturdy rejection of every form and degree of religious atomism. God speaks and the soul hears within the ambit of tradition represented by Scripture and the Church. Scripture and Church are organically united in one Word-bearing rôle, and he who hears the Word hears it through them only. But it is only *through* them that the Word comes to us. They are neither of them clothed with that infallibility which would make them simply identical with Revelation, with God's self-disclosure. The Word which through them finds us in the full response of faith is *in that response only* received and known by us as the authentic Word of God.

Now, no one, I think, will wish to deny the immense religious impressiveness of such a view of Revelation. It is all the more impressive that it has no immediate apologetic intention. It boldly assumes the religious offensive just where theology has for long grown accustomed to being on the defensive only. It not only sees no menace in the revolutionary results of criticism but welcomes them as the instrument which was needed for the complete elucidation of the revelational character of Scripture. For it criticism has been religiously constructive. It has justified and actualised the intuition of the Reformers that there were different grades of revelational value in Scripture, an intuition which had in its turn been anticipated and motived by the mediæval doctrine of the different grades of meaning. Revelation achieves its fulness as a self-disclosure of God in Jesus Christ, His Word as a Person. To this Revelation everything in Scripture—the ancient covenant with Israel, the prophetic witness to the coming Messiah, the words and deeds of Jesus Himself as a figure in History—is but a series of finger-posts at different turnings on the historical route. The nearer we get to the goal, the more important and significant these indications become. Scripture is in its entirety Revelation because from its beginnings till its close the Word proclaims itself as the Way by which we are being led. But the Word becomes clearer to us at every fresh turning of the Way which brings us nearer to its Personal utterance. To change the image, it reached us at first along the great ether wave-lengths in broken portions only. As we draw nearer we have no longer doubt that it is the authentic personal voice of the Word to which we are listening. From the beginning the word was sufficiently clear to awake the response of faith in it as God's Word. In the end the response it awakes is still faith, not vision. But it is now the super-faith that in the words and deeds of a historical person God is speaking to us directly as Incarnate Word.

It has been my main purpose throughout to show that the traditional doctrine of Revelation has all along left room for such a conception of developing revelational value in Holy Scripture. If it was not explicitly taught by the older theology, it was because it had but little occasion to consider the existence of a human element in Scripture. That occasion, however, the critical work of nearly two centuries has provided to the full. It is the claim of the Barthian theology that the work of criticism has for the first time clearly elicited the difference in revelational value which the older theology had somewhat haltingly admitted. That claim Anglican theology, too, and indeed English theology generally, has for more than a generation been urging in its own way with a growing measure of agreement. Yet there is a distinction in their ways of utilising criticism of which it is most necessary to take account. It may be said, I think, generally that English theology has been feeling its way towards a new apologetic and is all the time haunted by the consciousness that some modification in the traditional conception of Revelation itself may be rendered necessary. The Barthian theology, on the other hand, reasserts the traditional conception in the most uncompromising fashion, and is concerned with criticism only in so far as it believes it to have made the old conception both more possible and more fully significant. For it the human element in Scripture is separable from the Divine Word, and it is the service of criticism to religion that it has forced upon it the necessity of that separation. And yet we, our own unaided selves, are quite unable to make it. It is the error of the old fundamentalist orthodoxy to believe that no such separation is necessary, that the written word is to be taken just as it stands written, in all its parts and in equal measure, for the Word of God. Criticism, in exposing a very human element in every part of Scripture, has made such a position impossible save on peril of idolatry. If, on the other hand, we attempt the sifting process for ourselves we have no trustworthy and authoritative criterion of what is merely human and what authentically Divine. It is only God Himself speaking through the Scriptures so as to awake in us the response of a fully operative faith that can make them His Revelation to us. And if it be asked, " Why, then, should the Scriptures, being woven throughout of very human stuff, have the privilege of being the necessary medium of the Divine Revelation ? " the answer is that they are the human translation, with all the marks of their particular moment, of the one unchangeable Word which He spoke to those of old time as He speaks it to us now.

It will be conceded, as I have said already, that this reconciliation of religion and criticism is all the more impressive because it is not designed as a reconciliation at all, but is quite frankly the yoking of criticism to the chariot-wheels of religion. It is impressive because it is religion vindicated once more as Revelation, and as nothing but Revelation. But will it suffice? Let it be granted without the slightest nuance of reservation that religion as the bond between man and God is and must be of God's sole origination, that in all human quest of God God has been there beforehand to make the quest possible, that in the striking paradox of Pascal we could not be seeking for Him if we had not already found Him (that is, if He had not already found us), that Grace and Revelation stand for facts without which religion could not be. Yet in that bond man surely counts for something. For it is and must be a bond between persons. It may be answered, and indeed it has been the consistent answer of all pure Augustinianism, and only in a less degree of all mediæval theology, that it is that bond which alone and for the first time constitutes personality on the human side, that outside that bond man remains a loose congeries of unrelated and often conflicting aims and desires. But there must surely be in the natural man the stuff out of which personality is made. If grace is not a sheer miracle there must be some desire and even will to receive that which is given. If revelation is a real fact of the psychological order and not, again, a mere psychological miracle, then there must be some existent centre of at least incipient faith and hope and love awaiting the Divine self-disclosure as the supreme satisfaction of all these things. God may create a universe *ex nihilo*, but He cannot reveal Himself *ad nihilum*.

Jesuit theology has deserved well of the Christian

world in that it resisted so firmly the tradition of Augustinian intransigence and claimed a place for the natural man in the eternal sunlight if that light were ever to reach him. The Barthian condemnation of the claim to freedom of the natural man as his original and irremissible sin so long as it is persisted in, as a truculent rebellion against Divine authority, and its complementary conception of God as sheer unmitigated authority, seem to me the chief weaknesses of that theology, both psychologically and religiously. Psychologically, because without freedom personality of any kind is impossible. Even the freedom of the cubbish schoolboy who is kicking instinctively at every restraint is but a sign and accompaniment of the birth-throes of personality. And the natural man learns very early and very quickly that there is no freedom for him save within a circle of very narrow and very exacting dependences. It is surely just through this imperfect freedom that he can be, and most often is in fact, prepared for that ultimate dependence in whose service he finds the perfect freedom. And religiously, is not the Barthian conception a little too obviously at variance with the witness of Revelation itself? Even in the primitive stages of religion the Divine authority was recognised by Elijah not in the whirlwind and earthquake which in turn shook his mountain fastness, but in a still, small voice. And when at last God came to reveal Himself in the fulness of His eternal majesty, He left all visible majesty behind. There, to use the words of Bossuet again, what we see is human and very human, only what we believe is Divine. If the

Gospel narratives teach us any one thing more clearly than another it is this, that in Jesus Christ God spoke to us as men and with an almost inconceivable belief in our power of hearing Him as men. That God should tabernacle with men without ever declaring Himself openly, that He should to the last as it were jealously preserve His incognito, and yet trust men to recognise Him for what He really was, is surely an instance of belief in the spiritual capacity of man such as man himself would always shrink from claiming. But it is also the supreme revelation by God Himself of *how* He reveals Himself.

Now, these are facts which, it seems to me, we need to keep continually in mind in thinking out again the doctrine of Revelation as affected by Biblical criticism. We ought not to expect God to proclaim Himself either in or through Scripture with such a clear note of authority as He did not use in what we call His earthly life. As in Jesus Christ He was seen as man and yet believed in as God, so in Scripture He speaks throughout, but speaks throughout with a human voice or rather with many human voices. The human element in Scripture is not detachable from the Divine, because they were both concerned in the revealing process. For unless inspiration be regarded as the miraculous occupation by the Divine Spirit of its human instrument which would mean the mere suppression or coercion of personality, it must mean such co-operation of the Spirit with a human personality under the conditions of its actual receptiveness of Divine truth as will enable it to receive that truth with a dazzling clearness and a convincing certainty that it is of God.   In other words, personality in all its contingent actualness would seem to be the only means through which God can speak to us.   We may say that apart from actual communion with God there is no worthy and complete human personality.   But we must also say that apart from some incipient degree of personality there would be nothing for God to communicate with.   In other words, all intercourse between God and man is of the nature of an inter-course between persons.

Now, if this be admitted, it must surely follow that the Revelation which emerges from the fullest and most intimate degree of that intercourse will bear through and through the marks of its human recep-tion.   To adapt once more the phrase of Bossuet, what is heard is human, what is spoken is Divine. The Barthians are right in their magnificently religious insistence on the last clause.   We must hear God speaking *to us* in Scripture.   Otherwise it is not Revelation for us.   But we must hear Him also, just as those who first received the Revelation heard Him, from the midst of a personality which has had its slow and gradual growth, which through its growth alone has learned to hear.   We cannot believe in a mere cataclysmic act on God's part which takes no account of His own patient preparation of the hearing ear. That the effulgence of God's light breaking occasion-ally through the mists of human ignorance and hesi-tation and doubt in all its dazzling splendour must seem cataclysmic is true.   But it is also true that it was the same light which reached us, however dimly, through those mists.   And even when they are at length dispersed, it is still through our earthly atmosphere, tempering it mercifully to our needs, that the Divine Light comes or can come as our actual illumination.

The sum of the matter, therefore, would seem to be that Revelation cannot rightly be conceived otherwise than as the intensest form and degree of that general illumination with which God is present to the deepest needs of all His children and which He ministers to them through the whole world of experience in the midst of which their life is set. As St. Paul and Erigena and the mediæval Augustinians all alike held and taught, God's Revelation of Himself in Holy Scripture, culminating in His Revelation as His own Incarnate Word, is surrounded by a penumbra of preparatory revelation through His own created order. " The invisible things of Him from the creation of the world are clearly seen, being understood by the things that are made, even His eternal power and Godhead." History, too, had no value or even meaning for them except as a revelation of the *gesta Dei*. Cyrus was as truly His chosen servant as were Moses and David. To that rare insight, enlarged in its scope if, we must admit, also confused by our fuller knowledge of both nature and history, we must now return. It is in relation to these lesser revelations and to the manner in which we find God's revelation in them that Holy Scripture must in the future justify its claim to be God's supreme Revelation. Resort to the old credentials of miracles and prophecy has been, by the practically universal consent of our theologians, abandoned. Miracles are no longer " visible suspensions of the order of nature for a providential purpose," as they were for Mozley, but manifestations of the working of a higher law of nature as yet unknown to us. Revelation is no longer proved by miracles, but itself gives probability to them.

But in abandoning the evidential function of miracle we are abandoning also the rigorously traditional view of Revelation. That, again, Mozley placed beyond all doubt. " A revelation is such only by telling us something which we could not know without it. But how do we know that that communication of what is undiscoverable by human reason is true ? Our reason cannot prove the truth of it, for it is by the very supposition beyond our reason. There must be, then, some note or sign to certify to it and distinguish it as a true communication from God, which note can be nothing else than a miracle." The Revelation which is self-authenticating in the substance of its content, which needs no miracle to authenticate that substance, is brought *as to its whole content* within the ambit of reason, and is thereby something different from Revelation in the traditional sense. Theology is, I think, preparing itself honestly to meet this new situation. It is paying heed to Professor Whitehead's wise reminder that a religion which is not also a metaphysic, a reasoned account of nature and history as one whole, cannot live. The distinction of mediæval theology was that it satisfied that demand in very ample measure. Among the truths of Revelation it excepted only the Trinity and the Incarnation as completely undiscoverable by reason. But we cannot afford to except even them—indeed, them least of

all. Theology is now, as always, the science of Revelation. As such it must accept the truths of Revelation as the necessary first principles of its knowledge. But it must be able also to show forth those truths, and especially the truth of the Incarnation, as the absolutely necessary key to a world-view which will be more rationally consistent and complete than any rival view which proposes to dispense with them. There are signs that our younger theologians have recognised that this is the task set before them and are girding themselves to undertake it. It is a task at which many generations will have to labour before there can be much hope of satisfying accomplishment. We may remember for our comfort that it took many generations to carry through the work of criticism to its completion. The field is now open for the elaboration of a philosophical theology which will justify the Christian Revelation as the Divinely-given nucleus of the highest wisdom to which the reason of man, itself a reflex of the Divine Wisdom, can ever attain.

SYNOPSIS OF CHAPTER VII

Intelligibility of suspicion, whether among believers or unbelievers, of all attempts to restate doctrine of Revelation. Yet such attempts necessary in view of results of criticism. English theology specially prepared to make the venture by reason of its freedom in the matter of system. Attempt to exalt authority of Church at the expense of Scripture examined and convicted of radical inconsequence.

Necessary to examine more closely the meaning of Revelation in actual religious experience. All such experience comes as the impression of an external object provoking in man who receives it a uniform type of reaction and forcing him to ascribe to the Object a certain uniform type of character. This knowledge of the Object, immediately given, is the core of all specifically religious knowledge. Radical difference between this knowledge arising immediately out of an (analogically) personal contact and all inferential knowledge of the nature and attributes of a Supreme Being.

But knowledge arising out of a quasi-personal contact, the specifically religious knowledge of God, ought, it might reasonably be presumed, to grow in richness and depth. How then account for the arrest of religion, in some of its forms, at the most primitive stage of apprehension ? These forms would seem to represent man's premature satisfaction with the most elementary and unsifted impressions of the Divine Power which he has received from it. Yet the " periods of arrest " may also have a religious value if used to digest the knowledge received and prepare for reception of fuller knowledge from the same revealing source.

But what, it may be asked, is the criterion of values within the field of Revelation itself ? Without denying the part which the speculative and moral reason can play as such criterion, it is contended that ultimately the religious sense itself distinguishes what is Revelation from what is not and what is higher from what is lower. This contention illustrated and defended by the formation of the *Corpus* of Holy Scripture.

Final contention that revealed truth is of the nature of poetic symbolism, not of the clear-cut and sufficient statements of the logical reason.

VII. TOWARDS REVISION

IT would be useless to attempt to minimise the extent of the breach with the traditional conception of Revelation which a critical examination of the Scriptural documents has effected. It was natural enough that some such attempt should have been made, as it were, by the way, that theologians in being forced to accept ever more and more revolutionary results of criticism should have persuaded themselves and sought to persuade others that the essentials of the ancient conception had been in no way disturbed. Much of this provisional and almost haphazard apologetic was no doubt both legitimate and useful. Improvisation as it was, it may yet help towards the formulation of a theory of Revelation which will satisfy essential requirements of religion while making all necessary concessions to the findings of both literary and historical criticism. But meanwhile it is fully intelligible that to the popular mind such apologetic attempts should seem either self-stultifying or insincere. For it still believes that the traditional conception of Revelation is the only possible or legitimate one ; and it is supported in that belief by the fact that every orthodoxy, whether Catholic or Protestant, still tenaciously adheres to it.

The popular attitude towards religion may be one of belief or of disbelief in the truth of the Christian

Revelation, but in either case the sole, or at least the inclusive, motive of its attitude is its acceptance of the traditional conception of what Revelation is. The unbeliever is such because he thinks it unreasonable to ascribe to an infinite Truth and Wisdom and Goodness the authorship of writings which so often plainly offend against what even to us seems most assuredly good or wise or true. The believer, on the other hand, is a believer because in spite of all evidence to the contrary he is satisfied that God has once and for all revealed to man all that for his salvation he needs to know in the Scriptures of the Old and New Testaments, and that apart from that Revelation he himself could know nothing either of his own deepest needs or of the mode of their satisfaction. There may be the widest possible variation in his manner of using the Revelation which has been given to him. He may be a fundamentalist Protestant and claim the assured assistance of the Holy Spirit in his own individual interpretation of Scripture. Or he may be an observant and obedient Catholic recognising that assistance only in the interpretation of Scripture which the Church in her dogmatic definitions has authoritatively approved. But in either case his view of Revelation and of its necessity for his faith is the same. There is no fundamentalist Protestant who would not be grateful, if he had ever chanced to hear of them, for the firm pronouncements of the Vatican Decrees or the even stronger re-affirmation of their substance in Leo XIII's Encyclical of 1893. He could not ask for more than the determined assertion that the Holy Scriptures were written " at the dictation of the Holy

Spirit," and that they can contain no error because their author is the Supreme Truth itself. And Roman orthodoxy will not offer him less.

I

Now theology has, I think, in English-speaking countries more decisively than anywhere else broken with the old tradition. But it has done so incidentally and almost unconsciously. That the breach should have thus almost imperceptibly attained such wide dimensions in the course of less than two generations is probably to be accounted for partly by something peculiar to the English character and partly by something distinctive in the theological situation in English-speaking lands. But as the latter consideration is largely determined by the former, it may be sufficient to dwell upon it alone. In so far as the development of English theology has been influenced by movements within the Anglican Communion—for exception must be made in this regard for Scottish theology —it has been comparatively free from the trammels of any definite sacrosanct system. The only remnant of the scholastic system which the English Church preserved was its Articles. And even them, so long as they were used at all seriously as an instrument of theological instruction, it treated rather controversially than systematically. Their exposition was an occasion for making quite clear its rejection of rival theologies while leaving its own as nebulous as possible. This characteristic of the English Church may seem to some its chief weakness, if not its unpardonable offence against the plain duty of a Church to define with exactness the limits of Christian truth. Its own children have, on the other hand, seen in its instinctive shrinking from formal definition and in the greater liberty of speculation thus accorded to individual theologians the strength of a genuine loyalty to the Truth which, because Divine, all would admit to soar beyond the reach of every human definition.

This at least *is* the English tradition, deriving largely from the Erasmian impatience of Scholastic subtlety which was its earliest inspiration as an independent Church. It is, above all, a tradition rooted in the practical and unspeculative character of the English people as a whole. English theology seems to accommodate itself more readily than any other to the disturbing impact of fresh knowledge whether in its own or in alien fields. But the accommodation may be too easy to have permanent worth or validity, as I think has been the case in the matter of Revelation. There has, for instance, been a tendency among us to supplement the waning authority of the Scriptures by the authority of the Church. The Church, it is urged, gave us the Scriptures, and it is on the authority of the Church's ever-present living voice that we receive them now or ever have received them. It may not be sufficient, but it is certainly necessary, to meet this contention with the assertion that it is a complete theological novelty in so far as it goes beyond the assertion of a bare historical fact. It is, of course, a fact of history that the Church determined what Christian writings had a right to admission into the New Testament Canon just as it is a fact of history that the Synagogue had previously fixed the limits of the Old Testament Canon by selecting among the various prophetical and hagiographical writings to be added to the Torah. And for us moderns at least it is also a fact of history that the work of selection was in each case a very slow and gradual process.

But the consistent theological interpretation of these facts was that the primary rôle of Church and Synagogue was that of authenticating witness to the exclusive claim of certain writings to be of Divine origin. If both had also the subsidiary rôle of interpreter of the true meaning of Scripture, it was only as preserving what was believed to be the continuous tradition of such meaning. Their actual historical rôle was, indeed, what we conceive it to have been, that of a choice on grounds which, however little they recognised it, were really critical between documents in their possession. But their own conception of their rôle was widely different. It was merely to bear witness to the fact that certain writings were clearly of Divine origin while others were not, in the case of the Christian writings that some were of undoubted apostolic authorship while others falsely claimed that character. Once that authorship had been established for any writing, it took its place among the Christian Scriptures which beforehand had consisted of the Old Testament writings only. The contention, therefore, that the Church existed before the New Testament writings and that the latter are the record and confession of the experiences of the former, though historically sound and just, is theologically beside the point. The theological belief in the Church was that it came into existence in virtue of God's first communication of His saving will to man, that at the coming of Christ it had already been in existence for a space of four thousand years, that its history during all that time was the divinely determined fulfilment of the Divine Word originally spoken to the Patriarchs and repeated and reaffirmed at each of its critical moments, that that Word was (if I may put it so) finally translated into history in Christ as its own consummation, and as the consummation—not the beginning —of the Church which it had consistently heralded and prepared. That is the scheme of history as the traditional Christian theology has always understood it, and in this scheme the Divine character of the Church is clearly dependent throughout on the Divine Word of which it is the fulfilment. Its only authority is the authority deriving from that dependence. Its only legitimate claim to infallibility derives immediately and exclusively from the infallibility of Scripture.

The Christian Communion which has inherited in fullest measure the ancient theological tradition, in renewing its claim only half a century ago to be the exclusive representative of the Church thus conceived, reaffirmed at the same moment its belief in the infallible and inerrant character of Holy Scripture. If it had not done so, it would have been convicted of an illogical audacity of the highest magnitude. The Church which is not Divinely guaranteed cannot guarantee as Divine either its own character or that of any truth which it teaches. If, on the other hand, the truth which it teaches is Divine, it is so in virtue of its being the rightful custodian of an inerrant and infallible Divine Word.

Every attempt, therefore, to exalt the authority of the Church at the expense of that of Holy Scripture is not only illogical but suicidal. No Christian can think of or believe in the Church as a bare creature of history, and yet it will be increasingly difficult to show convincingly that it is much more than this if it is once separated from closest dependence upon the Divine Word which is, it is necessary to repeat it, for the orthodox tradition the inerrant and infallible Scriptures. Even for the New Testament Scriptures, whose actual redaction was by the clear verdict of history and, indeed, by the necessities of the case the work of an already existing Church, that tradition must maintain a logical priority on pain of an intolerable reduction of their revelational value beneath that of the Scriptures of the Old Testament. That it has, in fact, consistently done by distinguishing as a matter of course between the redaction of these Scriptures and their actual contents. What they contain is the original proclamation of the Gospel which fulfilled the Church of the Patriarchs and Prophets in the Church of Christ. And that proclamation of the Gospel by the Apostles and St. Paul was the embodiment of the Revelation made by Christ to the former by word of mouth, to the latter in vision. And that Revelation in turn consisted in the opening of their eyes to see in Him the fulfilment of " all that the prophets had spoken." In this scheme it is apparent that the mere redaction of the Apostolic Scriptures is quite secondary and subordinate and that the rôle of the Church as witness to the Word which constituted it, though important, is also secondary and subordinate.

Similarly, that the Church is " a witness and Keeper of Holy Writ," that the individual believer receives the Scriptures as a member of the Church and primarily —in time—upon its authority, is not only sound doctrine but obvious fact. It is, too, a doctrine as jealously asserted by the Reformed Churches as by the Great Church from which they were excluded. But it is also a doctrine common to the universal Christian tradition that " it is not lawful for the Church to decree anything contrary to God's Word written "— in other words, that the Church exists as the Church of God in sole virtue of its fidelity to His inerrant Word given in the Sacred Scriptures. If, therefore, the actual and legitimate authority of the Church in this regard is adduced as a sufficient substitute for belief in an inerrant and infallible Bible, the procedure is not only inconsequent but self-defeating. The Church cannot use its strictly limited authority to dethrone the power which gave and continually gives it that authority. I am not suggesting that any serious theologian has ever seriously committed himself to the maintenance of such a position. But undoubtedly language is often loosely used among us under the pressure of the critical assault upon the inerrancy and infallibility of Scripture, and especially in quarters where that assault ought to be most feared, which is gradually forming a habit of mind favourable to the adoption of this wholly delusive means of escape.

II

The fact that such haphazard apologetic devices serve only to make the problem more difficult and on traditional lines more insoluble is now forcing the theologian into a more radical examination of the whole traditional conception of Revelation. One point at least will remain secure and unassailable after the most rigorous and independent scrutiny of its claims upon our acceptance, viz. that Revelation is necessary to the very existence of religion. It may, indeed, be asserted in the most general way that all knowledge is primarily revelation, a self-disclosure of the object or of some aspect of the object known. Whatever elaboration it may be necessary for the mind to bring to the original impression made by the object, that impression remains as a regulative element in every further advance of knowledge. But in the case of religion the necessity of this self-disclosure of the object becomes something quite unique. There the object is itself so inaccessible to mere reason and yet leaves an impression so intimate to the deepest needs and secrets of our being that our knowledge of it seems wholly given. Further, our knowledge of the religious object seems to come to us not merely as the satisfaction of an existing need, but also as the creation or evocation of that need. And again, it comes not with the comparatively impersonal character of ordinary knowledge, but as a kind of personal bond which pledges us, with all we are or under its influence can become, to the service of the object. It awakens in us characteristic attitudes and movements of the spirit which are either altogether wanting or only remotely perceptible in the case of ordinary knowledge—sacrifice, veneration, prayer, unquestioning obedience and the like. And these attitudes, immediately evoked and imposed as it were by the object, become the means of all further knowledge of it. It is known only as it disposes us to know. Only in the case of religious knowledge does he who in any degree possesses it shrink instinctively from every claim to a share in its achievement. It has been simply given. He does not even call it knowledge, but faith. Its object has so disclosed itself as to leave the impression not of a something distantly or inferentially known but of a supreme and immutable truth which makes an irresistible claim to be believed.

Religion, therefore, without Revelation would seem to be in the strictest sense an impossible conception. Wherever religion has appeared among men, it has appeared as the knowledge of a Divine Object not laboriously achieved by them but communicated to them immediately by that Divine Object itself. In its higher forms, indeed, it has not only not denied but has constantly affirmed the competence of reason to attain to a knowledge both of the existence of God and of certain attributes which must necessarily be His. But it has never confused such knowledge with the knowledge which was peculiarly its own. Again, in reducing its knowledge to a system it has, it is true, utilised abundantly the results of philosophical reflection. Whatever reason has affirmed as necessary attributes of a Divine Being it has confidently accepted as true and turned to account in the construction of its theological scheme. But it has never attributed a simple equivalence to truths of reason and truths of faith, to the truth which comes from rational reflection upon Divine things and the truth which they seem of themselves to impose. And it has been justified in this distinction not only by the difference of the ways in which truth has come but in the difference in religious value between truth deduced by the mind and truth apparently given to it. To assert that God is infinite, unchangeable, incorporeal, impassible adds nothing to our positive knowledge of His nature. It does nothing more than state, with the aid of a negative prefix, certain incompatibilities of which reason becomes aware in its analysis of the idea of a Supreme Being.

Religion must take account of these deliverances of reason. It must even come to terms with them on pain of forfeiting its claim to be the supreme truth which gives them whatever significance they have. But that supreme truth which has been immediately given to it is of an entirely different order. It is the secret, not of an impersonal idea, but of a personal character. It affirms of God qualities which are altogether outside and beyond the cold pale of reason— that He is merciful, compassionate, gracious, forgiving, that He is redeeming love. Not only could the reason, in its affective aloofness, never have attained to such affirmations about a Supreme Being, but it has always been the chief difficulty of theology, *i.e.* of religion in working alliance with reason, to reconcile these metaphysical attributes of Deity with the strictly religious apprehension of God. And even where the intuitions of religion seem formally to coincide with the deliverances of reason, as in the ascription to the Divine Being of omnipotence, omni-science, &c. or even of moral qualities such as justice and truth, a difference of feeling-tone in each gives a quite distinctive significance to the same formal truth. Religion feels with the warmth and intimacy of a personal contact which shrinks from all analysis as a profanation what reason can assert only by deducing to its ultimate consequences in thought the necessary implications of an idea.

From every point of view, therefore, religion makes good its claim to be an autonomous sphere of know-ledge. Alike by the manner of its reception and by its positive content, its knowledge has a distinctive character which fully justifies its description as a revelation. But it is a long way from the recognition of this fact, a recognition which was never perhaps more complete than it has become in our own day, to any reaffirmation of the traditional theory of it in Christian theology. That theory was, as we have seen, that not only a unique but an exclusive Divine Revelation was given in the Scriptures of the Old and New Testaments, that it consisted in the communi-cation of Divine truth and was therefore infallible by its nature and inerrant in its formal contents, and that the Divine character and origin of this truth were expressly guaranteed in the Divine intention by the superhuman circumstances and powers in and through which it was communicated.

Now, quite apart from all question of the solvent effect of historical criticism, this theory seems to have the initial defect of at least confusing, if not absolutely denying, the revelational character of *all* religion. Yet this character is coming more and more clearly to be for us the specific difference of religious as contrasted with all other forms of human experience. We account all religions to be the revelation, the self-disclosure, of the same invisible Reality just because they all exhibit the same human reactions to its felt presence—awe, veneration, worship, the sense of an inner unworthiness which makes man loathsome to himself, makes him think of himself as unclean, the persistent need of inner purification expressing itself in agonies of self-chastisement, sacrifice, prayer, the sense of a strange guilt and of an equally strange deliverance from guilt, the shudder of a mysterious fear passing into the rapture of an equally mysterious joy. Religion is everywhere accompanied by these strange manifestations, among all sorts and conditions of men, among races representing the most various stages of culture, most widely sundered in time and space, moulded by the most dissimilar historical traditions. It is not necessary, as it would be obviously untrue, to contend that all men are equally conscious of these reactions. But what requires explanation is that, though always in any intense degree the monopoly of a few, they are yet so readily transmitted to whole multitudes, to practically all the members, whether of a primitive tribe or of a more civilised community, and are henceforth recognised by them as of sovereign importance for their own individual lives.

In the fact of these reactions, then, which universally

accompany and even constitute religion we seem to have the most conclusive evidence of its revelational character. Nothing less than the direct action of some invisible Reality can sufficiently account for them. And they do not only testify to its existence; they reveal its character also. It is, indeed, only in and through them that the distinctively religious attributes of God have become known to men. It is a knowledge to which the unaided reason could never have attained. Only these strange dispositions and attitudes of spirit which arise in us, the reason knows not how, force it to accept a knowledge beyond its range and foreign to all its characteristic moods. Reason may discover God in its own way, but its God has no significance for religion until it has been accommodated to the revealed knowledge which religion itself supplies.

The traditional theology, therefore, was abundantly justified in the clear-cut distinction between the revealed knowledge of God and all knowledge of Him which man could attain through rational inference on which it so strongly insisted. It failed only in not grounding the distinction sufficiently in the nature of religion itself as it has always and everywhere appeared among men. Its failure is readily explicable when we remember two facts. Firstly, however subtle and often profound was the general human psychology of the Schoolmen, they had never felt the need of a distinctively religious psychology. And secondly, loyalty to the Christian Revelation as Divine Truth seemed to them possible only by drawing the sharpest distinction between it and all other forms of religion, a distinction in which the one appeared as infallibly true and all the others as utterly false and delusive. It was only by the theory of invincible ignorance that the salvation of men outside the Christian fold, which even human ideas of justice demanded, could be provided for.

But explicable as the failure of which I have spoken may be, it has had disastrous results for the theory of Revelation itself. On the one hand it was forced to find the criterion of Revelation not in its religious content, not even in the manner in which it was apprehended, but ultimately in certain miraculous circumstances which attended its deliverance. And, on the other hand, it made faith primarily a belief that the Holy Scriptures are the exclusive Divine Revelation and only secondarily and dependently a belief in their religious content. It reduced Revelation to dependence on an external, accidental and debatable circumstance, and faith to an acceptance of it as Revelation on these external, accidental and debatable grounds. And it did this through its refusal to recognise the obvious fact that all religion is either an illusion which just happens to be universal or the operation of a single Power upon the souls of men which evokes in them all a characteristic reaction and through that typical reaction evokes in them also a common type of belief in the character of the Power, a belief which is primarily, however much it may be rationalised afterwards, extra or supra-rational.

K

III

But it is clear that any theory of Revelation which starts from this intrinsically revelational character of all religion must account for the vast differences which distinguish the most primitive religions from those that we rightly account the most highly developed. For these differences are quite obviously differences in revelational value. Even though religion everywhere brings men to their knees, uplifts their hands and their hearts in worship, turns their eyes inward and beyond to see the invisible, and reveals the God Who has compelled them into those attitudes as awful yet gracious, as righteous yet merciful, as exacting yet forgiving, as Judge and yet Redeemer, and so forth— yet no sane person will maintain that these attitudes and these beliefs, in spite of their similarity, in spite of their witness to a common cause, are of equal revelational value, that there is no difference in the depth and wonder of the Divine Nature which are disclosed through them to an African tribesman and a Christian saint.

Now the problem which is here presented would seem to be not so much how to account for the development of religious knowledge as how to account for its apparently arbitrary arrest at certain times and among certain peoples. If we assign to revelation that universal character which both the nature and the universality of religion seem to require, if we conceive of the characteristically religious attitudes and impressions of the human spirit as the necessary result of the continuous action of the Divine Spirit upon it, and if

further all our distinctively religious knowledge of
God arises immediately out of those attitudes, if, in
other words, that knowledge comes as an immediate
divination of the nature of the Cause which produces
effects so mysterious yet so intimate, we ought surely
to expect a continuous growth in that knowledge.
For it is a knowledge which even in its most primitive
and rudimentary stages has transformed man's nature,
if only by turning his gaze from the things that are
outside and around him to the things that are within
and beyond. And with that transformation we
should expect an ever greater clearness in man's vision
of the ultimate Reality, a steady growth in his apprehension of the admittedly inexhaustible secrets of its
nature. But this is very far from being the case. The
existence, for instance, of tribal religions to-day wit-
nesses to the lifelong arrest of religion at its most
primitive stages. It might, indeed, be possible to
account for these arrests by indifference or even
deliberate resistance on man's part to the Power which,
ex hypothesi, is working upon him, though such an
explanation might seriously call in question the universal character of religion as revelation. But as
matter of fact such indifference is met with at all
generally only where religion exists in its higher
forms, and may be then something quite other than
what it seems.

Religious indifference among primitive peoples is
not only rare but in the strictest sense impossible. For
the most primitive reactions to the Divine Power, the
most primitive apprehensions of the Divine Nature,
are there at once hardened into a system of propi-

tiatory ritual acts by which the very life of the tribe
and therefore of each individual member of it is supposed to be guaranteed.   The growth of religion as
revelation is arrested just because the first rude and
unsifted impressions of the Divine Power are accepted
as final and sufficient.   And these moments of arrest
reappear throughout the whole history of religion
wherever new and deeper impressions of the Divine
Power, new and fuller apprehensions of its nature,
are being reduced to a system of belief and worship
which make them more easily assimilable by the multitude.   These periods of arrest, therefore, have their
undeniable value for religion.   But if persisted in
beyond their point of usefulness, they become its
greatest danger.   They destroy the revelational character of religion in affirming of their own system that
it is the final and complete Divine Revelation.   They
deny what is for religion the most fundamental
character of God, His nature as *Eternal* Word,
Eternal Revealer, in their jealous affirmation that He
did speak, *did* reveal Himself, once, in a past which is
past.

Amid the abundant merits and services of dogmatic
theology is this one serious demerit and grievous
disservice, that in its righteous zeal to defend the
uniqueness of the Christian Revelation it made it also
exclusive and infallible, and thus tended to reduce, if
not altogether to annul, belief in the essential character
of religion as man's ever-present learning of the things
of God from God's ever-present action upon him.
Against this tendency mysticism, and especially
mysticism in its most typically Christian forms, has

been a constant and not ineffective protest. We might say the only protest, if we did not remember with gratitude Zwingli's revival of the intuitions of a Justin Martyr or the contention of the seventeenth-century Jesuit Cardinal de Lugo that men could be saved not on the grounds of their ignorance of the one exclusive Truth but by their positive obedience to the measure of Divine truth revealed to them through their own religious tradition.

IV

But one question, or rather group of questions, of the most crucial importance remains for Christian believers who may be inclined to adopt the theory of Revelation which we have just been discussing. That theory implies that there is and must be a largely, even prevailingly, human element in all Revelation. It will always be refracted through the prism of our humanity. Even those few whom God whispers in the ear hear with ears which are all-too human. And when the pen and the tongue come to translate the language of that whisper, the message of eternity is still further tempered to the transient, ever-changing moods of time. But further, the eternal message does not always merely endure the necessary and inevitable reductions of time. It voluntarily condescends to time. God speaks to the need of a particular moment, and especially in the Old Testament is that character of His Revelation everywhere apparent. It seems as if it might be so easy here to confuse what is authentic Revelation with that which can make no claim to such a character, so very difficult to make the distinction with any confidence or certainty. How, then, are we to distinguish what is Revelation from what is not? And how are we to distinguish one Revelation from another as being, as it were, less diluted, less refracted from its Divine original?

To the first question the old theology had a ready answer, an answer which had the advantage of forestalling and foreclosing all inquiry into the detailed contents of Revelation. Only one feature of the contents of the Old and New Testaments had to be recognised in order to secure their title to be integrally and exclusively the Word of God, viz. the miraculous accompaniments and the miraculous medium of their delivery. The test was so far accidental and external, and has besides become for us so questionable as to be no longer available. Yet it had, too, another character which gave it a deeper probe. The miraculous circumstances of the Revelation were not disjointed and separate and so merely external to the revealed Word itself. They were a continuous Divine Act, God's continuous action upon and through a particular people, preparing a fuller and fuller disclosure of His will of redemptive love towards man up to the personal revelation of that will in His Incarnate Word. This is a reading of the Divine purpose in history which every Christian will gladly accept if only he can persuade himself that even the main outlines of the history of which it is a reading are true to fact. That, indeed, is more difficult for us than it was for the Christians of former generations. But even for them it did not of itself serve as the sufficient guarantee of the exclusively revelational character of Scripture. On the contrary, belief in this revelation of a Divine purpose in history was for them motived by that same accompaniment of miracle which enabled them to accept as inerrant and infallible Revelation the Scriptural Canon as a whole.

We must resort, then, to some other test of Revelation. Physical miracles, even if we could be assured of their actual occurrence as recorded, seem to us too remote from the substance of Revelation to be a sufficient guarantee of its reality, more especially as history is full of recorded miracles which have no connection with Revelation. The only test we can apply is the verdict of the religious sense itself. If, as we have contended, religion is—at any rate in its moments of most vivid awareness and greatest intensity—the spontaneous and fully conscious response to a Divine activity, it will, we may believe, even in what I have called its moments of arrest, retain some power of distinguishing its own peculiar type of truth. Even those in whom the religious sense is atrophied, and to whom the substance of the Revelation therefore means nothing, will at least recognise that what it offers as truth is at any rate not an acquisition of the discursive reason. They will at least be able to apply negatively to the manner of reception of what claims to be religious truth the very same test which the religious soul or the religious society applies positively both to the mode of acquiring it and to its actual substance.

Now, judged by this twofold standard there is probably no collection of writings which are more consist-

ently stamped with the hall-marks of revelation than
the Christian Scriptures. The mere fact of their
collection, indeed, into a single *corpus*, however it was
accomplished—and the more gradual and as it were
accidental the process, the stronger will be the testi-
mony—bears witness to the existence of this religious
sense and the sureness of its perception in the highest
possible degree in all those who were responsible for
the selection. With the possible exception of parts
of the Wisdom literature, there is here no truth which
could have been acquired by cool reflection upon the
known facts of human life and nature. Everywhere
else in Holy Scripture we are confronted with a different kind of truth, different still more by the mode
of its apprehension than by the character of its content.
It is truth gained by an intensely vivid and never fully
analysable personal impression. It is the record of
this impression in its first full ecstatic glow before the
work of analysis begins, where, indeed, all conscious
analysis would be felt as a desecration. What the
subject of the experience has felt and known in the
experience is ascribed in its entirety to the Divine
Power through which it has come. He himself
counts for nothing in its reception. He knows only
that it is God who has spoken, commanded, forbidden,
that it is God who is uttering His sovereign will, who
remonstrates, pleads, reasons, persuades. He himself, indeed, in his turn pleads and remonstrates, but it
is only that he may hear and recognise the more clearly
that decisive Word of God which puts an end to the
controversy.

This revelational character is sealed upon every

page of Holy Scripture, is as evident in the Prophets
as in the Torah, or again in those very primitive
religious conceptions and practices which are to be
found in the Book of Judges as in the Gospel declaration of the mystery which had been hidden since the
foundation of the world. And yet the miracle of the
Bible is not the mere fact that it has this character
throughout, but the further and strictly astounding
fact that it embraces under the one head of revelation
and in the same revealed *corpus* every form and expression of religion, from conceptions of the Divine
Nature and of the kind of worship it requires which
do not materially differ from those current among
primitive tribes to-day up to the sublime monotheism
of the Prophets and their profound spiritualisation of
the worship of God, nay up to the mystery of God in
Christ as it was apprehended by the religious genius
of a St. Paul or a St. John. The whole religious
education of the human race is here seen in God's one
eternal moment. The slowness, the gradualness, the
endless vicissitudes of the process are in these pages
manifest to the modern historian of religious ideas as
in no other single collection of religious records. And
yet no one of its many writers ever thinks of his message as a development from anything that had gone
before. It is the one truth which God had spoken
so often and is speaking again through him, and he
seems quite unaware of the fact which is so clear to
our critical eyes, that it testifies of itself to the inadequacy or unworthiness of revelations which had preceded it in time. And where, as in the discourses
placed in the mouths of St. Stephen and St. Paul by the

author of the Acts of the Apostles, there does appear
something like what we should call a philosophy of
history, it is used only to vindicate the more clearly
the identity of the Revelation which has been repeated
by God throughout the whole course of history.

We see in the history of Israel what we somewhat
lamely call a progressive revelation, by which we
mean, I suppose, a historical process whose Divine
character is revealed in its Divine consummation and
only by reason of that consummation.   But the
Biblical writers, even where they were as historically
minded as the writer of the Acts seems to have been,
had no thought of development in that sense.   The
Divine purpose had been revealed *in its integrity* to
Adam, to Noah, to Abraham, to Moses, at the very
beginning of history.   God, indeed, used Israel in the
fulfilment of His purpose, but He took care to reveal
to it from the beginning—indeed, before *its* actual
beginning—the knowledge of that purpose without
which it could never have been its efficient instrument.   In other words, revelation was not a perception of Divine truth emerging, however convincingly,
from some particular process.   On the contrary, it
was the antecedent Divine revelation of that truth
that had given the process its unique character.   It
was the continuous repetition of that same identical
Revelation which kept, and alone could keep, the process true to the Divine purpose in it.

It was natural, therefore, that the New Testament
writers should appeal not to the impression which the
life of Jesus had made upon them, which was no doubt
the real motive of their belief in Him, but to the fact

which they regarded as evident and self-substantiating that His life was the fulfilment of prophecy, for the fully convincing proof of their belief. It was natural, too, that the Old Testament Prophets should never for a moment have suspected that their teaching represented a religious advance upon that of their predecessors or have betrayed the slightest sense of a difference so obvious to us. It was natural because they conceived of the life of their people not as a progress in its knowledge of religious truth, but as a continual backsliding from that knowledge. When they uttered their woes and condemnations against the apostasy of Israel, it was not in virtue of some new truth which God had spoken for the first time in and through them. They were only repeating—so at least they thought—the same truth which God had so often spoken already through His servants, the truth, indeed, whose possession had first constituted Israel God's people and loyalty to which could alone preserve for it that character.

Such facts as these seem to point to the conclusion that there are as it were two distinct moments in the development of religion, the strictly revelational moment which constitutes it and the moment of reflection which recognises and canonises its own revelational content. As expressions of the essential nature of religion, these moments are not to be considered as mutually exclusive. To receive a revelation and to distinguish it afterwards from what is not a revelation are both evidences and effects of one and the same self-revealing Power, even though the former may have a priority of religious value over the latter. But in the history of religion they do seem to be successive in time. It was only when Israel felt that the era of immediate revelation had been completed that it heard the call to fix the limits of its Revelation and set a protective hedge around it. It was not until everything that could make a reasonable or even remotely plausible claim to be accounted apostolic tradition had been committed to writing that the Christian Church set itself to the task of fixing the New Testament Canon. In both cases the tests of genuineness which were consciously applied were mainly historical, questions of authorship and the like quite foreign to the religious judgment. But we must, I think, hold that it was the inspired certainty of that judgment which really guided the choice of both Church and Synagogue. At least the fact remains that modern historical criticism has seen good reasons for suspecting or even rejecting the validity of the tests which they applied, while the religious judgment of the Christian Church to-day confirms *ex animo* the validity of their actual choice and reaffirms that choice as its own.

V

English theology seems for a generation or more to have been moving steadily towards some such theory of the nature and tests of Revelation as I have here tried to indicate. I cannot at any rate interpret otherwise its now customary insistence on the autonomy of the religious experience, its claim, that is to say, that religion has an exclusive right and competence to recognise and validate the truths which belong to its own domain. If that claim is meant to be a new kind of defence of all the positions and necessary consequences of the traditional conception, it plunges us at once into sheer irrationalism—and that quite gratuitously, since the tradition in its systematically developed form will certainly be neither able nor willing to accept its aid. But of itself it need be nothing more than the statement which seems incontrovertible, that essentially religious truth and knowledge are of a quite distinctive type which may be characterised negatively by saying that they are not results of any process of the logical reason, and positively by saying that they are impressions of the nature of an invisible Power or Order beyond us arising, apparently, out of the immediate action of that Power or Order upon us. And if this is what is meant by revelation *in genere*, then it would seem to follow that all religious knowledge is revelational in character and that since we can distinguish degrees of truth-value in religious knowledge it must be in virtue of some intrinsic test, itself of a revelational kind, that we are able to make that distinction.

There is therefore so far no slightest breach with the traditional belief that the Scriptures of the Old and New Testaments are throughout of Divine Revelation compact, and that the knowledge given in this Revelation is of a kind to which the discursive processes of man's unaided reason could not possibly have attained. The stress here is laid, of course, on the word " unaided." It is not suggested that man's reason is as it were excluded from the scope of that Divine action upon him in virtue of which he perceives truth as revealed ; but that it is so included in that action as to lose all sense of an independent activity of its own in such perception. The truth issues directly from the Divine impression upon a nature which is essentially rational, and yet could never have been acquired by that nature apart from such an impression. " They shall all know me from the least of them unto the greatest of them, saith the Lord ; for I will forgive their iniquity and I will remember their sin no more." Here there is an implied knowledge of the Divine Nature which is no doubt an inference of the reason, but it is of the reason rapt up into a complete unconsciousness of itself by the wonder of the Divine impression of forgiveness. Yet it is not necessary that in the reception of every truth which has a right to be called revealed the reason should thus lose all awareness of its own action. It is necessary only that its activity should be dominated throughout by an overmastering sense of its mere instrumentality. It is receiving, not merely seeking, even when it seeks. " In that thou art seeking Me, thou hast already found Me." The limits of Revelation must be sought in the limits of this receptive attitude of the mind. Where the mind has passed on to independent reflection upon the truths of Revelation, it has crossed the border-land into theology. Jeremiah is as clearly Revelation as the Athanasian Creed is not.

And it is therefore just at this point that, however reluctantly, the decisive breach with tradition must be made. For it held quite definitely that the kind of knowledge which Revelation gave consisted in exact, clear-cut truth-statements. It was an immediate communication of truths as they existed in the Divine mind, even though their communication might involve some measure of accommodation to the human mind's power of reception. The fact that the actual revelations of Scripture had very seldom anything approaching this character was for tradition something of a scandal, a difficulty which had to be explained away, as, for instance, by a Divine purpose to keep the human mind more alert in its attitude of reception. For us the difficulty does not exist. The scandal becomes the clearest witness to what we should expect in man's attempt to translate the knowledge he had received through God's immediate action upon his rapt and expectant soul. The effect of that action upon man is to exalt him into a mood of perception in which the mind is as it were dazed by the wonder revealed. Through figure and image and symbol it translates the awed impression of a truth whose vastness and sublimity must ever elude its clear grasp. The typical medium of revelation is not the thinker but the seer. The revelation as received is not infallible truth caught in the net of clear, sufficient, inerrant statement, but an intimate personal certainty too great for words which are not possessed by its own transfigured glow, too bewildering as yet for the thought which would reflect and weigh and measure and formulate. It is not the literal truth which is only possible as the last refinement of the critical intellect, but the symbolical truth which transcends all the cold processes of the reason.

Inerrancy, infallibility, and the like are only ideal limits for the acquisitions of the human mind, limits which it must always pursue yet can never reach. They may indeed be applied to Revelation as honorific terms to remind us that the knowledge which it gives is the result of an immediate impression from the Supreme Truth. But to Revelation as received they do not and cannot apply. By the transcendent greatness of its subject-matter it must be received in "divers portions," with an imperfection which can never be wholly overcome. By the inspired contact with the Divine Nature which is the mode of its reception, it is received in "divers manners" and always through the symbolic and therefore intellectually inadequate translation of vision. The peculiar majesty, the sovereign authority of the Christian Scriptures are not to be sufficiently characterised by speaking of them as infallible, but perhaps by describing them as classical. They are the classical Revelation of Divine Truth not only because in them we ascend to the topmost peak of Revelation in the Incarnate Word, but also because they mark every step and stage of the revelational ascent. In them the Spirit has led humanity into all the truth of God, beginning with its most primitive apprehensions and ending in the Fulness which can never be exhausted by the fullest human apprehension of it.

*Made and Printed in Great Britain
by Hazell, Watson & Viney Ltd.
London and Aylesbury*